Confidence is a much sought after, yet rarely understood trait. It's fundamental to success in most of our endeavors. But rarely is a path to becoming more confident laid out so clearly. Tim reveals such a real-world, everyday path, drawing from vast leadership and coaching experience to share the stories of real people as they stepped into their confidence, bringing to life the lessons you too can use. And, as someone who has spent my career teaching and training coaches, I appreciate how Tim incorporates an educational and application component at the end of each chapter to ensure you will walk away with clear steps and tangible outcomes.

D. Luke Iorio
President, Institute for Professional Excellence in Coaching (iPEC)
and One Idea Away

Every day I work with entrepreneurs to help them grow their businesses. I want it to be fun and I want these individuals and their companies to be better versions of themselves. What Tim has captured in this book aligns perfectly with my vision of success for my clients. He focuses on the human side of leadership and how working on those "softer" attributes propels the leader forward to effectively execute the systems and processes to become extremely profitable. Entrepreneurs and established leaders will benefit from the insights Tim shares, and will be able to immediately feel the impact on their lives both personally and professionally.

Charles Gaudet
CEO, Predictable Profits

Tim Ressmeyer's thought-provoking book offers a unique no-nonsense practical approach to learning the top qualities of leadership. The Impact of Confidence offers you the ability to uncover or elevate your leadership growth opportunities! It's a must read!

Jesse Ferrell
Author of *How You Leave Them Feeling*

The road to becoming a successful, impactful leader often includes many daunting obstacles and annoying detours. But author Tim Ressmeyer provides virtual GPS navigation in this book to guide readers on the correct path. Adhering to these proven strategies can bring out the very best qualities in all of us.

Fred Mitchell
Professor, Author,
Former Chicago Tribune sportswriter (41 years)

In my work with tens of thousands of coaches at all levels, I am always looking for resources that help show the value of coaching. The Impact of Confidence does just that. Tim's ability to show through real-life examples the way that coaching helps leaders overcome obstacles is a brilliant contribution to our profession. His focus on the human side of leadership, and not just tactics, is done in a way that makes you confident you can become a better leader.

Benjamin Croft
CEO and Founder WBECS

Tim understands what all great leaders do; empathy is everything. Whether you're a team leader, or a Fortune 500 CEO - achieving success is about understanding what your peers need from both you, and themselves. As a CEO, I know first-hand the value of taking a human-centered approach to leadership, and I attribute a lot of my success as a leader to Tim's teaching philosophy. This book captures his approach well, and I recommend it to anyone wanting to improve their own skills as a leader.

Scott Kitun
CEO, Technori

It is a rare book that moves the reader from insight to action. Reading The Impact of Confidence: 7 Secrets of Success for the Human Side of Leadership is like engaging a package of coaching sessions. The reader is changed by the insights, tools, and exercises unveiled in each chapter. From the first page to the last, Tim elevates a vision of leadership rooted in caring, connecting, growing, and taking control of your life. Add this book to your library and reference it often!

Steve Ritter
CEO, Team Clock Institute

As my coach, Tim has been enormously helpful to my personal and professional growth over the past years. His book is like having a mini-version of Tim that I can carry with me every day.

Lisa M. Dieter, CFP®
Founder & Wealth Advisor, EmberHouse

Leadership. MATTERS! If you are a parent, you are a leader. If you are a colleague, you are a leader or you CAN be. If you are a volunteer, you are a leader or you SHOULD be. Leadership comes in many flavors.... And there is a HUGE difference between LEADERSHIP and power...and THAT'S why Tim Ressmeyer's book is a MUST read. The anecdotal style covers many leadership styles and dilemmas...and you will likely see yourself in a few of them. In this book The Impact of Confidence: 7 Secrets of Success for the Human Side of Leadership, you can HEAR Tim's voice, as if he were sitting across the table from you. He is a coach that will guide you and inspire you to YOUR best self, to finding your leadership style. It's a delightful read that will sharpen the lens of the vision you have for your career, your family and your future.

Amy Coveno
Chairman, Court Appointed Special Advocates – NH
WMUR-TV

In my journey from corporate marketing executive to international keynoter and consultant, I've faced many challenges, many fears... some successfully and others not so much. What I now know is that each of us has an opportunity to be a great leader, to be the CEO of our lives, to grow and to stretch and achieve dreams beyond our wildest dreams, and Tim's book is the map that charts that journey. Each chapter delivers a critical life-lesson wrapped in a relatable story that will inspire you to action. I was particularly moved by Tim's exploration of self-trust as a means to move forward... a powerful lesson I continue to learn over and over. My life's purpose is to teach people how to generate demand for who they are and what they do, and that can't happen without confidence; this book is officially on my recommended reading list going forward.

Sima Dahl, CSP
International Keynote Speaker & Consultant

As leaders, we employ our knowledge and our relationships to build our organizations. Building, sustaining, and repairing relationships call on us to be aware of our own energy and passions, as well as those amongst the members of the team in which we work. Tim Ressmeyer's coaching has been so valuable to me as a leader in building relationships and helping our team thrive. As I read Tim's book, I see his voice and style come through. This book is an excellent resource for leaders wanting to develop their own skills while managing a host of complex interactions and career transitions.

Sacha Kopp, Ph.D.
University Dean

I am confident that the reader will be blessed, challenged, and affirmed by digging deeply into Tim's new masterpiece! It is personal, professional, passionate, poking, and provoking. His writing style is such that I felt like I was having a personal conversation with the author himself! Unlike some "Leadership" books, this resource is not just theories, quotes, and "how to's" for the professional consultant and executive, but is also a practical resource for the parent, the pastor, the educator, and to all others who want to make a difference in this world of today. Thanks, Tim, for the impact your life and writing has had and will continue to have on people like myself, and on so many others. And one more thing: I'd like to add one more "Secret of Success" to your list of Seven – and that is for us readers to tell others about your new book so it will not remain a "Secret" very long!

Dr. Rich Bimler
Ambassador of Health, Hope, and Aging
Ministry Consultant

Tim brings an embraceable approach to understanding how confidence works in your total life - at work and home. Furthermore, reading this book will give you the confidence to have confidence! You well be pleasantly equipped to better serve others and yourself in all types of situations.

Mike Cacicio
President, Make It Happen Now

Tim Ressmeyer is an empathetic guide on the leadership journey we all travel. Drawing on a lifetime of professional experiences and astute human insights, Tim's advice is good for careers and good for the soul.

Tom Barritt
Partner, Ketchum Public Relations

A must-read for people across all industries and disciplines, from executives to students, The Impact of Confidence will inspire individuals to harness the necessary confidence to enhance every aspect of their careers and everyday lives.

Gregory Sharp, Ph.D.
Assistant Professor
State University of New York at Buffalo

The Impact of Confidence:

7 Secrets of Success for the Human Side of Leadership

Timothy J. Ressmeyer, Ph.D.

First Edition Design Publishing
Sarasota, Florida USA

The Impact of Confidence: 7 Secrets of Success for the Human Side of Leadership
Copyright ©2018 Timothy J. Ressmeyer

ISBN 978-1506-906-49-2 HC
ISBN 978-1506-906-50-8 PBK
ISBN 978-1506-906-51-5 EKB

LCCN 2018947615

July 2018

Published and Distributed by
First Edition Design Publishing, Inc.
P.O. Box 20217, Sarasota, FL 34276-3217
www.firsteditiondesignpublishing.com

"The Ride," from *Home/Body* by Georgia Ressmeyer, Pebblebrook Press, copyright © 2017 by Georgia Ressmeyer, is reprinted with permission.

Photos by Christina Wehbe Studios

Library of Congress Cataloging-in-Publication Data
Ressmeyer, Timothy J.
  The Impact of Confidence: 7 Secrets of Success for the Human Side of Leadership
/ written by Timothy J. Ressmeyer.
    p. cm.
    ISBN 978-1506-906-50-8 pbk, /978-1506-906-49-2 hc. /978-1506-906-51-5 digital.

1. BUSINESS & ECONOMICS/ Leadership. 2. / Personal Success. 3. Skills.

T3744

To my Dad,

The Reverend Doctor Bishop Rudolph P.F. Ressmeyer
Or, how everyone knew him,
Rudy
From you I learned how to be a Leader with faith,
integrity, compassion, and confidence.

Acknowledgments

I want to thank my parents, siblings, and children, Emma and Ethan, who have created the support and experiences to lead me to where I am today. I appreciate the Institute for Professional Excellence in Coaching (iPEC), for providing stellar coach training, and Conversational Intelligence® / The CreatingWE Institute that uses cutting-edge neuroscience research in understanding how we interact with one another. The learning from these two organizations permeates the insights throughout this book, and I strive to honor the integrity of their work. I thank and am humbled by my clients who daily trust me as they share their hopes, fears, accomplishments, and challenges with me. Together we uncover the ways to move forward to find success, happiness, and fulfillment. Many of their stories are woven throughout this book, and names have been changed to honor the confidentiality of our relationships.

And, I thank my wife, Kerri. Without her support, love, and confidence in me, I never would have been able to make the leap into following - and living - my passion as a coach.

Foreword

Even though I make my living writing and sharing ideas, every now and then I come across something so powerful I feel that I don't have the ability to adequately communicate its impact. That's how I feel about this book. I've spent the last 30 years of my life, traveling all over the world, to help people and businesses become more successful. I have worked with hundreds of companies and read literally thousands of business books and I am truly in awe of how well Tim has captured this collection of truly life-changing ideas.

The 4-C's model you're about to learn is elegant in its simplicity, yet one of the most insightful frameworks I have ever seen about the fundamental elements necessary to be a highly effective leader in both your career and personal life. As you move chapter by chapter through the "Seven Secrets," you will discover a path for how to create more confidence, impact, and happiness in your life. I was especially pleased to see how Tim has balanced the importance of having abundant confidence in your skills and abilities, without ever letting it slip into arrogant confidence. It was also interesting how this book challenged me on both intellectual and emotional level, pushing me to think deeply about how I wanted to improve as a leader and as a person.

Through a series of stories and examples you're going to learn some very important business and life lessons. However, no matter how valuable the ideas are, they are worthless without implementation. At the end of every chapter there is a section called "Taking Action." I want to challenge you to complete all the exercises and answer all the questions. I can absolutely guarantee that if you invest your time and effort to do the activities, the ROI will be stunning.

Tim has dedicated his life to helping people become better leaders and has spent years putting all his best ideas and advice into this book for you. Take this gift and use it wisely, for it can change your life and the lives of all you touch.

I wish you every possible happiness and success,

John Spence
Top 100 Business Thought Leader

Contents

Introduction

One of my earliest memories of my Dad was hanging onto the clergy stole that draped over his robes on Sunday mornings. I'm sure it was super annoying for him as he greeted parishioners as they left the church to have a four-year-old tugging on and playing with the fringe at the end of his vestments. The worship service had ended, and all I wanted was to go home. It was a large suburban congregation on Long Island in the early 1960s, so there were hundreds of people to whom to say goodbye.

No matter how bothersome I was, he never lost his cool and made sure he could focus on his conversations with the adults. He had an important role that I could not appreciate as a very young child. Way before I was conscious of what was going on, I was seeing my Dad as a leader.

All these people listened to him preach, teach, and counsel them. He had a staff at the church and the adjacent Lutheran elementary school who looked up to him to be their boss. And there were hundreds of children in the school who saw him lead chapel services on weekdays.

He left that role when I was still quite young to take on the position of Executive Director of Long Island Lutheran High School that he had helped found just a few years prior. We lived on the campus, and I could visit him in his rich wood-paneled office. The title, the responsibility, and his seeming ease in leading created a vision of leadership that exuded confidence long before I knew there was any other way to lead.

A few years later he came home and said, Tim, "You're now truly an S.O.B." Startled, I had no idea what he meant. He explained I was now a Son-Of-a-Bishop. He had been elected to lead hundreds of congregations in the New York City area as their spiritual and administrative leader. It was a title he held until his retirement more than 20 years later.

I admired and learned so much from him as I moved forward with my career.

I always wanted to be a leader, and my Dad was my first and compelling example of what a leader can look like.

He passed away at the age of 93 on October 6, 2017. He had been retired for nearly 30 years. The last six months were difficult to watch as the man I always admired deteriorated physically while mentally remaining strong. He was fully cognizant of his circumstances. We had sustained conversations about all sorts of things. Being a man of faith he was ready for the promise of eternal life, and being reunited with those he loved.

Things happen in our lives. It causes our paths to change. We look at things differently. We make choices. We move forward confident we know where we're headed. We get surprised; not so sure we're on the right path. We look back, and we say, "How did I get here?"

Sometimes those things that cause a course shift are big and obvious, sometimes small and subtle.

Life is not linear. Life is not predictable. Those things that happen impact us in ways we don't fully realize in the moment.

My Dad dying during the writing of this book was one of those pivotal moments. I do know the immediate impact. My insights into what I learned about leadership from him took on new meaning amidst the sadness and loss. I couldn't talk to him about such things anymore, and I would write about them.

I don't know the long-term impact of his death. It didn't mean a course change, but rather an opportunity to help understand more fully the path I'm on that was now mixed up with a new reality.

His example of leadership was faith-based and included confidence that God would lead him to what was next in his career/vocation. He never set out a plan to run a school or become a Bishop. This absence of goal-setting runs contrary to typical career advice and goal-driven planning. At various points along the way, job opportunities would present themselves, and he would discern what the right next step would be. This "strategy" had a significant impact on my approach to career development.

He had always hoped that either my brother or I would follow in his footsteps and become pastors like him as well as his father and grandfather. We didn't, and yet he was always supportive of the work we did. In retrospect, my path has resembled his in that I have been open to opportunities as they presented themselves, shown the confidence to step into new areas to use the gifts I have, and strived to make a difference in people's lives.

My Path to Leadership

Years later and after the completion of my Ph.D., I landed a job at a major market research firm in Chicago. For personal and professional reasons, I had opted to leave academia and the life of a faculty member. I wanted to apply my research skills, be a leader, and make an impact in the business world.

It was my first corporate job. I was so excited. My doctoral advisor told me the salary for my first job out of grad school was the highest a graduate of the Political Science Department ever received! I was working in downtown Chicago, had a nice office, was part of a team, and had a direct report. Things were great, and I felt I was on the right path.

I came into the role confident with my research skills. After all, I had been doing quantitative research since my sophomore year as an undergrad, had completed a master's degree, and had spent five years as a faculty member doing research and teaching social science research methods. I had recently finished writing a 250-page dissertation using some of the most sophisticated statistical techniques at that time. I know this stuff.

A few things happened over that first year that led me to doubt my decision, and I wasn't sure I was in the right place.

I was in a consumer research group at the firm, and within the first few weeks found myself sitting in what was called a Lead Team meeting. There were about 15 people from groups across the company, including account management, technology, sales, etc. talking about the work we were doing for our client. We worked with top-tier consumer packaged goods companies so it might have been Frito-Lay, Procter & Gamble, Pepsi, or another big name. My portfolio of clients was pretty broad. The goal of the Lead Team was to continue to service clients and grow our contracts. We would do that by helping them be more successful in selling their products to consumers.

I was there representing my group, and I had no idea what they were talking about. I prided myself on knowing a lot about a lot of things, and being a fast learner – but I was lost when it came to this subject matter. All of the marketing tactics, retailer relationships, and product development strategies were beyond me. I wasn't sure of the contribution I would be able to make being so in the dark. I took the position of listening only and then trying to figure it all out afterward. I certainly didn't want to be called on by someone in the meeting and have to come up with a profound answer to a question on the spot.

It was all different in this new world. There were different data sources, tools, and ways of presenting results. In academia, research projects would last for months or even years. In corporate, clients wanted to have results in days or weeks. I knew I had to come up with answers; I just didn't know how to make it happen with this whole new language of methodologies and expectations.

I also felt like I had to do it all myself. Having been hired in with a great title and salary (at least compared with what a junior political science faculty member would be making), I felt responsible for knowing everything and doing everything.

I had to deliver reports to clients that would help their businesses and to convince them to buy more research from us.

I also had to manage Greg, the analyst I inherited. He was a brilliant guy and didn't really fit the image of a corporate employee. He played in a rock band and looked like it. Hair, clothes, tattoos, language all fit that rock star brand. He often came to work late, spent time booking concert tours over lunch, listened to music so loud in his headphones everyone could hear it anyway and drove me crazy by getting projects done barely under the wire. We also traveled together to our clients. My father always taught me to be at the airport early. Our family joke is he always left enough time to get to the airport to not only fix a flat tire on the way but with enough time to rebuild the transmission. When traveling with Greg, he was typically the last passenger on the plane – as the door was being closed. I'm sure they were paging his name back in the terminal that his flight was ready to leave. I was already in my seat nervously wondering if he would make it on board, and anticipating what our meeting would look like in case he missed the flight. I was struggling trying to figure out how to work with him, and whether we could really do the work we were tasked with. I was questioning my abilities as a leader in this new environment. Then, things began to change.

I approached my boss, Laura, and came clean that I had a lot to learn about this new industry. She was willing to answer all my questions. She would invite me into calls she was leading to help me learn her approach to addressing client needs. She helped me navigate the internal politics and structures. It became clear that my background and research skills were in fact right in line with what was needed, and my outside perspective was extremely valuable to create new ways of serving our clients. I just needed her to connect some of the dots for me.

Through the course of this mentoring, I uncovered a particular research methodology that I thought was hugely impactful but was being underutilized by our group, so I helped to reposition and revitalize it. My passion for delivering results for our clients with this tool became well known throughout the company, and our sales increased.

I also mustered up the courage to work more effectively with my peers. The feeling I had to do it all on my own wasn't working for me, and I quickly found that connecting with them, getting a clear understanding of the work each of us was doing, and looking for shared success helped all of us. We created a tight group of exceptional researchers and business experts who were delivering great work. We found ways to work together so that we were all contributing to the greater success by tapping into each other's unique skills and abilities.

We were having a profound impact on the rest of the company. People from account teams across the company were looking for our expertise and passion for helping them with new and existing clients. We were being invited to conversations and opportunities rather than having to track them all down ourselves. And, other employees were asking to join this group because of the quality of work and energy of the team. People wanted in on the professionalism and fun!

There was still Greg. I wanted to improve my management skills, and this was where it had to begin. As a leader, it's awkward to have to address the more personal concerns. After one business trip, I had to have the sit-down talk with him to use a dry cleaner or at least iron his clothes. The I-was-out-till-3am-look really wasn't working when we were visiting clients who were still wearing suits and ties. I realized he didn't like barely getting things done on time either, so I worked with him on his time management and prioritization skills. He also worked aggressively to complete all of the documents we needed for client meetings enough in advance that I would have copies in case he didn't make the plane. He never missed a flight.

I also began to trust him and focus on what was right and not what was wrong. He was an astute analyst who saw things in the data that were invaluable to clients. I got out of his way and gave him more responsibility in articulating and presenting those results. Our client teams loved him and knew he did great work, so I didn't stress over his rock star style of interacting. I learned to help him play to his strengths, and I didn't dwell on the things that were not essential to his and my success.

My boss/mentor left the company a year or two after I started. Her replacement came in from outside the company to take over our team. We had been growing significantly, and clearly were on a high trajectory. One day his boss and his boss's boss came into my office and closed the door. Not always a good sign.

They didn't take any time in saying my new boss had left the company after just a year. They wanted to promote me to Vice President and lead the group. I was floored. I had not seen it coming. I said yes.

Everything I had been learning in those first couple years had laid a fantastic foundation for the team I was now running. My peers yesterday were now my direct reports. I felt confident in my leadership skills, and we saw terrific success. Our team continued to grow in both headcount and revenue; both of which doubled over the next few years. One year we took on a challenge from senior management that if we increased our revenue by a significant margin, they would pay for a team trip to Las Vegas. The goal was so high, the exec I shook hands with on the deal never thought we could do it. We more than beat the goal and had a great time in Vegas.

During this time, and throughout the eleven years with the company, I learned vital lessons of what it takes to be an impactful leader. The confidence to know what I brought to the table *and* it's ok to ask for help was a valuable learning. I wasn't always the smartest person in the room – and didn't have to be. I had a team for a reason, and helping them play to their strengths created an atmosphere of success and fulfillment that led to quality of life and quality of work. I was the leader, and we still worked together as a team. The value of looking at each person as an individual, helping them play to their strengths to overcome obstacles, and supporting them as they built the career they wanted was personally and professionally rewarding.

I left that company and spent another decade honing my leadership skills, having ups and downs in both my personal and professional life, continuing to be open to where my path would lead me, and being open to choices as they became evident.

The L Train

One of these choices led me to my career as a professional coach. I was enrolled in a coaching and leadership development course and was riding the L train in Chicago to my job where I was still working as a Senior Vice President at a prominent advertising agency in the Loop. It was early in the morning, and as I looked around the CTA car, I was struck by the lack of optimism and confidence all around me.

There were tradespeople with their coolers, hard hats, and rugged work boots with years of paint or caulk or whatever embedded in the leather. Service providers of all ages heading to the hotels, restaurants, hospitals, or office buildings wore the shirts or jackets embroidered with the name of their companies. There was a cadre of workers coming off the night shift at O'Hare airport with their dangling lanyards representing airlines, TSA, or other support companies. Younger employees were on their way to the co-op workspaces, tech companies, or Fortune 500 corporations re-establishing a presence downtown. A few mid-to-late career folks like myself, were ready to shoot up high-speed elevators to the lofty heights within the downtown skyscrapers. Individuals were sprawled out and occupying pairs of seats. Clearly they had been there overnight with nowhere else to go or had made a choice to sleep in the train until asked to leave.

As I looked around the train, these wildly different people had one thing in common: passiveness. Their indifference was evident by frowns and hunched shoulders. Eyes were distant or closed, certainly not making eye contact. No one engaged with each other or the world around them. The only movement came when there was shuffling to make room in the adjacent seat when a newcomer joined this train of detachment.

There was little expression of confidence that they were looking forward to the day that lay ahead of them.

I realized that I was seeing every single person in a way differently than before. It felt as though a clouded piece of Plexiglas was lifted from my eyes and now everything was crystal clear. I had seen these postures before, but what struck me was that in virtually everybody on that train car I saw melancholy, disappointment, or at best just blah.

Why? Why do we have to go through life like this? Is this what our God, divine being, or the Universe intended our life to look like?

That morning confirmed my decision to fully embrace my path as a coach to help individuals be happier, more successful and fulfilled in all aspects of their life.

We are all leaders. And we are leaders of ourselves first and foremost.

I learned this tenet early in my coach training and continually share it with others as I describe the philosophy that drives my coaching practice and purpose. You become a leader of yourself when you realize you have more control in situations than you thought. The same thing can happen to six different people, and those six people can all respond differently. The barista messes up your order at Starbucks. How do you react? The client has pushed back on a decision to buy your services until sometime in the future. How do you respond after hearing that challenging news? How might someone else respond? Your responsibilities in that new C-level role are significantly different than you thought when you accepted the offer. How do you show up now?

The Impact of Confidence

When I'm asked, what number one challenge my clients face, I can, without hesitation, say it's confidence. Whether they're freshly minted in the workforce or a seasoned veteran who has seen success, confidence continues to be a challenge and opportunity for *everyone* to feel more comfortable as they continue to achieve success and fulfillment.

Countless hours of coaching individuals at all different stages in their lives, has shown me that a willingness and ability to *step into your power as a leader* is the number one indicator of success. Failing to do so is the number one cause of a lack of success, and the number one cause of those emotionless bodies on the train. Confidence drives the ability to show up as a leader.

Confidence is often unevenly distributed in people's lives. Some might lack confidence overall and struggle at work and in their relationships. More often than not, they are highly successful in parts of their lives, but something is holding them back in others. There's likely a cause of that hesitancy, and by uncovering why and learning the tools to move forward with impact is life-changing.

I started my own coaching company after a 30-year career that included time working within nonprofits, academia, and 20 years as an executive in market research and advertising companies.

Parts of that story are incorporated in the chapters that follow. My personal story winds throughout each chapter, as do the experiences I have had professionally working in business both as a leader and professional coach.

One of the many things I love about coaching is the rapid change it brings. I see the very dramatic change in my clients all the time. We do look at your past and identify events and experiences that might be holding you back. We don't have to stay there too long, though. You also have to go to work tomorrow. You have to have a difficult conversation with your child. You have to make a significant business decision.

Amazing things happen in the coaching session, and even more magic happens as clients leave and realize the connection, insights, and tools are making a difference as they go back into their world.

Over the last few years of his life, my father was very intrigued by my coaching practice and asked lots of questions. He showed a different and more profound level of curiosity than he did when I was in the corporate world. He indeed saw it as a form of service, even though it wasn't as an ordained minister. A couple of months before he died, he asked if I would accept his clergy ring when he died. I wear it proudly thinking of the example of leadership he provided.

He showed confidence as he moved through his career, and faced his death. Passing along his ring was an indication of the confidence he had in me for the work I do.

Confidence supports and underlies everything we seek in life.

Seven elements that are fundamental to your personal and professional growth comprise each of the chapters that follow: Leadership, Passion, Connecting, Transitions, Advancement, Relationships, and Control. Looking at each of these through the lens of confidence allows you to identify how you can achieve more. You will find success and fulfillment while having fun along the way. Finally, there is a chapter on the Four Faces of Confidence that creates an accessible framework to help you decide how you want to show up in the experiences you will encounter.

I want this book to help challenge you to see the leader you are, the way leadership shows up in your life and how you can become the leader you want to be. And it all begins with confidence.

Chapter 1

The Confidence to Lead:
The 4 C's of Leadership

*Leadership and learning are
indispensable to each other.*
John F. Kennedy

*You should be doing
what you uniquely can do.*
Tim Ressmeyer

I've seen – and experienced – the highs and lows of successful leadership.

Sometimes you feel you're on the top of your game. You're in the flow or in the zone. You can take on any challenge, and you are confident you will be successful. Whether it's coming up with a big idea, leading a client meeting, or telling your boss why you want that promotion, you feel like you can do anything. And sometimes that confidence is so much harder to come by.

Sometimes you feel you can connect with anyone. Whether in networking, selling, communicating or managing, you feel you can form relationships that work to your benefit.

And there are times you feel you're just not clicking and no matter what you do you can't seem to create the relationship you want or need.

You know what it feels like when someone comes up to your desk and asks a complicated question, and the answer rolls right off your tongue. You remembered the content and how to solve the problem and recalled it brilliantly. You're in the flow. You know your stuff and were able to apply it. That feels good.

Alternatively, there are those times when you're in over your head. Knowledge of the subject matter is no longer as easy as it was. Whether more was expected than planned for your role, or you just didn't keep up with the necessary expertise, your competence is not adequate for the task at hand.

Finally, sometimes you know you're in an environment where everything is clicking. The ability to play to your strengths because your skills are valued, feedback is handled constructively, you see a career path, or you know you are making a difference is all part of a culture you long to be part of.

There are, however, too many situations where people feel the culture is toxic. There is so much negativity; going to work is not only uninspiring, but it can be physically painful. And you don't seem able to make a difference.

Over the course of my leadership and coaching career, I am convinced these four components, Confidence, Connecting, Competence, and Culture create a framework to understand leadership that leads to success. The leader who can look at themselves through this lens – and are willing to dig deep into the elements of each – will discover a holistic path to fulfillment both personally and professionally.

Leaders who get out of their own way, put themselves on a professional growth track that is based in the authenticity of their strengths and values, are willing to learn and trust as they go, and draw from the energy of those around them are the ones who *will* succeed.

Matthew had just moved into a senior management role and was thrilled with the title, responsibility, money, and opportunity to grow with an innovative company. In his mid-30's, he was confident this was the right move for him and his family, professionally and personally.

He hired me as his coach when things began to unravel after a couple of years in this role. He came to me angry and afraid. Angry that what he expected from his boss and the company hadn't materialized. He felt the promises made where not being honored. Bonuses were not as large as anticipated or being paid out in a timely fashion. He felt new criteria for the payouts were being made on the fly; the goal posts were being moved. His reviews included a lot of positives for his professional capabilities, but there was a lot of conflict on his team for which he was being held accountable. His relationships with others on the leadership team were spotty. He had his allies, but others were not willing to work with him in the ways he felt would bring about positive change.

His home life was challenging as well. As a husband and father of a young child, there was stress inherent to the relationship with his wife and as a parent. He traveled a fair amount, and his work commitments occupied a great deal of his time as well as emotional capacity. He wanted to be a good dad, and the increasing negativity at work was impacting his ability to do just that. Likewise, carrying that stress into the workplace was not helping him deal with the ever-increasing pressures.

Matthew was losing confidence in his ability to be the executive and husband/father he wanted to be. There were fractures in his capacity to connect and build healthy relationships at the office and with his family. He was losing a willingness to listen to others and see things from another point of view. His anger and resentment were compromising his competence in his role, and he stopped doing the full range of professional activities he was good at. He blamed the toxic environment on others, feeling the culture was tilted against him.

He began to question his own ability to have an impact, stopped connecting with people he didn't get along with, started to not deliver against his strengths, and he blamed it on the culture. He wanted out of his job.

When prospective clients come asking me to help them "get a new job because it's horrible where I am," I tell them with that kind of a mindset they're not ready for a new position. You don't want to go on the market angry or desperate. I assure them a new job might be in your future, but right now we're going to work on you. The goal of coaching at this point is to set yourself up for success whether you move on or stay where you are.

With a significant amount of work together, Matthew began to realize this perspective. He knew it wasn't just the culture. He realized he would have to make changes in his approach. Otherwise, the same cycle would repeat itself. He wanted to break the cycle.

He realized how he was showing up wasn't working and he wasn't the leader he wanted to be.

In my coaching practice, I focus on these 4 C's of Leadership when creating a custom program for clients. For each of the areas, we evaluate the current state using assessments and discovery as necessary and set goals for moving forward to achieve personal and organizational goals. Coaching serves to: uncover the obstacles that are in the way, teach new ways to approach challenging situations, support effective and newly learned behaviors, applaud results, and build in the motivation for continued success.

Matthew's situation provides an instructive case study to see the importance and interplay of the 4 C's.

Confidence

Confidence is the way an individual "shows up" in every aspect of their professional life and is a key to success. Executive presence is built on confidence, and without it, the highest levels of success are not achievable. The focus is on identifying individual leadership strengths, and how these are manifest in normal and stressful situations. Then, through coaching, the leader can uncover what's holding them back and to learn the tools to present themselves in the most impactful manner possible.

Clearly articulating your viewpoint, standing up for yourself, or knowing what you want to do next, are the critical steps towards confidence.

Leaders benefit from active confidence. On one end is a passive confidence where you expect everything to work out and you don't try. Indeed it is a *lack* of confidence, and you are willing to let the current take you where it will. The other extreme is an arrogant confidence where you bully your way through life never learning from others and always feeling you have to be right. The most effective confidence is that which gives the leader the ability to step into any experience and create the outcomes they desire with the people and situation at hand. It's not always easy, and you don't know exactly what the outcome might be, but you are willing – and confident – to step in and create something amazing.

Matthew had lost confidence in his ability to continue on the career path he was truly capable of and had worked so hard to create. He had lost clarity as to where he wanted to go professionally. He felt handcuffed to a particular company because of both financial and ego-driven reasons. He was falling into the trap of starting to look for a similar position at a similar company. He was also fighting a tug to revive his entrepreneurial spirit from his college days. He had always wanted to run his own company and even had a plan sketched out for what that might look like. He didn't know how to sort out a constructive path forward.

Having muddled goals and a lack of confidence in his ability to control his world was playing out negatively every day at work. He tried to manage his team and be a leader in the company, and it wasn't working. His performance was not at the level it should have been for his role. The way he was interacting with his direct reports, peers, and the management above him were not up to his capabilities. He was also struggling to be seen as a leader across the larger organization.

He was falling into a pattern of blaming others and not believing in his ability to take charge of his destiny.

Matthew's role was highly visible. He had to be able to show that his work had a cross-functional impact, and he would frequently deliver presentations to groups across the company. We had been working together for a while when one of these speaking engagements was coming up. Matthew knew this was one of the places at work he wanted to break the cycle of frustration and blame of others for the way he was feeling. We talked about how we wanted to show up for his speech, and equally important how he wanted to feel *after* the speech. When you decide what you want to feel as you leave the stage, it helps you stay on track during your talk. "If I want to feel calm at the end, why am I allowing myself to get stressed out mid-speech. That's violating my goal. What can I do to get back on track to stay calm?"

We were focusing on his confidence. He described the negative energy of the people to whom he would be presenting. He saw them as the enemy and felt they would be non-responsive to his message to such an extent he told me he imagined them with BB guns aimed at his head during the presentation! They were looking to him to fail, and he was on the path to letting that happen.

We talked about the value of his speech for the company, how important it was, and how accurate his perception was about the hostile crowd. I pointed out you can't control other people, but you can control yourself. If you show up expecting to be attacked, guess what, that's what you'll get. You are not at your best if you have that sort of expectation.

Matthew set goals for himself before and after the presentation, and we discussed ways to reframe and get through the real and imagined obstacles he was anticipating.

Matthew texted me in the evening after he had delivered his presentation,

> *Hey! Presentation was a solid A. Feel exactly how I hoped and envisioned I would feel. Great feedback so far and feels very good. Was a good test, as the energy level in the room was very low most of the day. I was surrounded by negativity but found a way to rise above and do my thing. Felt very good.*

Reestablishing his confidence as a presenter helped Matthew take a step forward in a critically important aspect of his job, and gave him a much-needed boost as he looked to move forward.

Connecting

Connecting is not just about how to communicate, it's how you connect with others. Whether it's your boss, senior management, colleagues, direct reports, clients, or vendors, research confirms the way in which we build trust with others allows us to achieve success, or to create barriers unnecessarily. Specific tools are utilized to help the leader engage with others to increase their ability to connect most effectively.

People have an inherent need and desire to connect with others. There are neurochemical processes in place that help facilitate connecting, and others that resist connections when there are perceived threats. As a leader, you are served by being aware of the behaviors you engage in that either hinder or encourage connection. Failure to be mindful of this obligation on your part to help foster connecting with others leads to barriers that inhibit the formation of relationships that lead to creativity, problem-solving, and growth.

Matthew's ability to connect with others had deteriorated significantly. He was so focused on his situation, and perceived everything as contrary, that he could not even find ways to foster impactful relationships with others. He was judgmental and mistrustful of those around him and was therefore unable to work towards collaborative solutions to the work that needed to be done.

One of the particularly difficult interactions was with his boss. He respected and admired his boss, but was finding fault with her on a range of issues. There was uncertainty across the company, and Matthew wanted reassurance he would "be OK" no matter the outcome of the changes. Even though he knew he was not performing at his best, Matthew craved validation regularly from his boss that he was doing well.

As he became increasingly self-aware that his work was subpar, Matthew began to distance himself from his boss. He didn't want to hear the realities and thought the best way was to work in his world and limit conversations as much as possible with his higher-ups. It's a normal tendency, whether conscious or not, to withdraw and become passive when you're not doing well, and you just want to avoid interacting with others.

We discussed the impact of this place into which he had drifted. Of course, he knew it was not sustainable to have this relationship with his boss, yet he was scared he would be called out on not working at the level she knew he was capable of. He was embarrassed.

We talked about ways to reconnect with his boss. There was still mutual respect; there was just a fraying of the relationship. Matthew decided to hit it head-on with his boss. He looked for the opportunity to have a professional conversation where he shared that he knew he could be a stronger performer than he had been. Rather than only worrying about himself in the context of the changes in the company, he showed empathy for his boss's situation by asking what he could do to help strengthen her position. And finally together they arrived at action steps to keep him on track and accountable for improved performance.

Reestablishing his relationship with his boss helped Matthew to also look at his relationships with his direct reports and peers. Feeling better about connections in one aspect of your life can help inspire them in others as well.

Competence

Simply stated, you have to know stuff. Subject matter expertise, time management, organization, sales, and productivity are among the array of skills a leader has to be able to have in their toolkit. Not every person has to be a master of everything, and certain benchmarks must be attained at an intermediate level, while others indeed have to be exceptional. Understanding roles and required competencies, skills training can be incorporated into a development program to ensure the leader has access to the tools to help them succeed.

Concerning competence, Matthew was willing to continue to use his comprehensive toolkit of skills to meet the needs of his role and the organization. He did run the risk of losing the motivation to stay relevant and overall was able to avoid this pitfall of not contributing to meet at least the essential competencies of his role. He was not, however, in the place of working hard to increase what he had to offer his company. Failure to grow in a position will not lead to long-term success.

When I moved from a role in a more traditional market research company to a senior analytics role in an advertising and digital media company, it was a real awakening about the need to keep learning and be relevant. It was at the time when digital marketing was taking off, and it seemed every week there was a new data source we had to figure out how to measure and integrate into our analytics. Our clients wanted to make sure we were capturing as much information as possible, and because big data was exploding, there was a lot of data of which to make sense. New programming tools were becoming prevalent and I knew nothing about them. As a senior exec, I didn't have to learn how to code in these languages, but I was definitely at a disadvantage not knowing them, and I had to learn and understand them as much as possible to be able to effectively lead my team.

During this time, I was approached by people from the same traditional market research firms I had experience with who were looking for jobs. I very quickly addressed their assumptions that "data is data," and "as long as I know the tried and true programming language, I'll be fine." The world had changed. I encouraged them to use the passion for learning that had gotten them to this point in their careers, to take the opportunity to dig into the new data sources and tools that would be necessary for this new era.

The Millennial v. Boomer debate in the workplace helps to illuminate the importance of understanding competence as a critical leadership characteristic.

Using *extreme* stereotypes, Millennials can be seen as coming into their roles thinking they are already experts because they have always won a trophy just for showing up. Whether they have an education to back them up or an "entire year of experience," they feel they should be rewarded and promoted. Their value is so evident, things should fall into their laps, and they will learn enough new stuff as they go along, and they will decide what those areas of focus will be.

Millennials have come-of-age in a very different culture than Boomers who were raised by the generation who had lived through the Great Depression. There is a much different understanding of a work ethic that leads such success. It's not necessarily right or wrong; it's just different. Boomers who criticize Millennials should realize they're the ones who raised them and taught them their values!

Stereotyping Boomers or the "old timers" in the workforce also highlights how competence can be viewed differently. Resisting change or new technological advances because "we never did it that way before," suggests an unwillingness to learn new things. A reluctance to take that course, get the next level of certification, or listen to the podcasts indicates a complacency that will not serve you or your organization. Taking an active approach to expanding your areas of expertise not only keeps you sharp and interesting but raises your value in the marketplace where being "old and expensive" can be a challenge.

This is not to say that the older members of the workforce have to learn everything new that comes up. Looking very carefully at your role and seeing where you can grow, contribute, and stay relevant is the lens you want to use to decide where to increase your competency. Be very self-aware when you slip into the trap of dismissing a new technology or methodology. Ask yourself whether you are ignoring it because it's confusing, too hard, or truly not an essential asset to your professional or leadership toolkit.

Allowing the newcomers to an organization to inject new energy with new competencies – especially around technology – can be something that can be embraced and not seen as a threat. Seeing experienced employees as resources for expertise, institutional history, and understanding the highs and lows and trend shift over time, allows for stability that mitigates fear and impulsiveness.

Examining these multigenerational groups as an example shows that competence in the workplace is defined differently, and continuous learning as a norm for the leader is essential.

Culture

Whether you are the leader of two or 2,000, you are creating a culture around yourself. Creating an environment of how you act and react is an intentional effort that "doesn't just happen."

In Matthew's situation, he was blaming the culture for a great deal of his dissatisfaction and unhappiness. He was condemning his boss and the style of leadership being modeled as the cause of all the problems. He fostered a feeling of righteous indignation that legitimized Matthew's disgust and anger toward the organization.

Unfortunately, Matthew was also reinforcing and furthering the culture that was so frustrating for him. He was interacting with the leadership and his team with negativity and withdrawal. He was initially not self-aware enough that he could, in fact, create a culture around him *in spite* of the culture that was in place.

So often I hear clients complain that they work in a difficult or toxic environment. I agree. I've been there. I have worked in places with very challenging bosses and where there were structures at the top of the organization that did not support what I believed to be very fundamental principles of good management.

I realized I couldn't change the culture of the entire company. I could have an impact on what I did have control of, my team, and every person with whom I interacted. I could create a culture around myself that aligned with my values, and what I believed was the way people should be treated.

At one point in my career, I was managing a group, and my leadership team was comprised of about eight people. It was in a young and innovative company where there was a highly competitive sales culture, and the environment fostered – and allowed – a significant amount of judgment, negativity, gossip, and demeaning of others throughout the company.

Although the company was growing, my belief is this type of culture is not appropriate (or necessary) in a professional organization, and unfortunately, it's all too prevalent. It reduces productivity, and an inordinate amount of energy is wasted due to petty, personal, and unprofessional behavior.

This culture permeated the team I was responsible for when I arrived. I could have tied in and let it continue, but I knew it was hurting our productivity, morale, and how the rest of the organization – and our clients – were viewing us. I did not want to be just like the rest of the company.

I elected to have a sit-down, face-to-face conversation with each of my direct reports. I delivered the same message to each that this kind of behavior is better left to the junior high playground, and has no place in this group. We discussed more impactful ways of using competition to achieve goals that do not include putting other people down or gossiping. We agreed that disagreements or poor performance could be handled directly with the purpose of finding solutions rather than using it as a mechanism to embarrass.

Virtually each of my team members thanked me for my decision to hit this head on. They didn't like the culture that had been, either. These were good people who had been raised with the Golden Rule, or the parental guidance, "if you can't say anything nice, don't say anything at all." Nonetheless, they were nasty towards co-workers. There was an immediate culture-shift within our team, and the impact of positivity improved our quality of life and began to impact our cross-functional partners and our work product.

One team member didn't understand the problems I had raised. He was, in fact, responsible for a great deal of the negativity. The subsequent conversations with him helped him know that he could be more successful if he shifted his way of working with others on the team and across the company.

The remainder of this book details how confidence can assist a leader in their path to success.

TAKING ACTION

The Four C's of Leadership Wheel is below. Each of the 4 C's is represented by two attributes of each of the four areas. More dimensions can be included to even more fully uncover your leadership growth opportunities, and some of those wheels appear elsewhere in this book.

Consider each of these components of leadership:

CONFIDENCE
Articulating a Viewpoint – Ability to state clearly and confidently my point of view

Clear Goals – Having a good idea of where I am headed and how I want to get there

CONNECTING
Listening – Focused attention to what the other person is saying

Collaborating – Ability to engage with others to create results and solve problems together

COMPETENCE
Knowledge – Having the requisite subject matter expertise to do my job well

Continuous Learning – The ability and desire to add to my knowledge base to stay relevant and successful

CULTURE
Trust – Ability to create an environment of trust with those I work with

Conflict Resolution –Ability to resolve conflicts with those I work with

STEP 1:

IMPORTANCE - Score yourself on each of the dimensions. Number 1 is not at all important to me, and 10 is extremely important to me.

Answer these questions:

> ➢ How hard was it to score yourself?
> ➢ What surprised you about the results?
> ➢ What patterns do you see across the dimensions of what are or are not important?

STEP 2:

SATISFACTION – Now look at each the dimensions again. This time score how *satisfied* you are currently with each of these dimensions. Number 1 is not at all satisfied, and number 10 is extremely satisfied.

Answer these questions:

> ➢ What surprised you about the results?
> ➢ Where do you see the biggest gaps?
> ➢ What patterns do you see?

STEP 3:

ACTION PLAN – Now that you have seen both the importance and your satisfaction with each of the dimensions, you can set a plan for what you want to focus on. It's hard to tackle everything at once, so you might look for one or two areas to start working on right away. It may be where the biggest gaps are between Importance and Satisfaction, or it might be an area that's really been bugging you, and you know it's time to tackle it.

> ➢ Make a list of 2-3 dimensions you want to focus on.
> ➢ What would the value be if you improved the satisfaction by just a couple points?
> ➢ What would it take to improve my score?
> ➢ How do you want to do that and by when?

It can be very typical that these scores be different if you are thinking about your personal versus professional life. Feel free to complete the exercise separately for each. After doing that ask yourself why is different, and what can you learn from one part of your life to impact the other.

FOUR C'S WHEEL

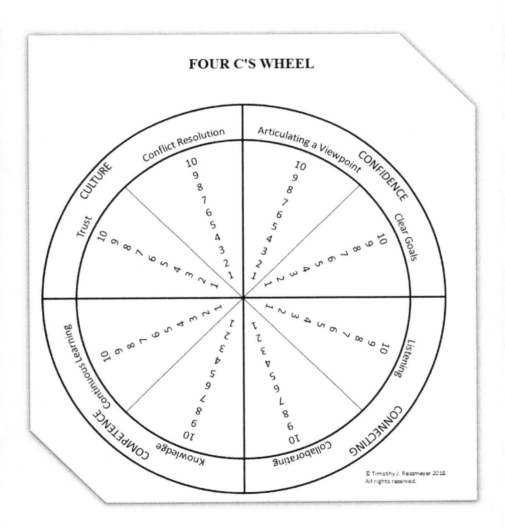

Chapter 2

The Confidence to Dream: Uncovering Your Passion

*It is obvious that we can no more
explain a passion to a person
who has never experienced it
than we can explain light to the blind.*
T. S. Eliot

*I know I can do it,
but do I want to do it?*
Tim Ressmeyer

There's so much loose talk out there these days about doing what you're passionate about and how not to dread work. "Quit your job and pursue your passion." "If you do what you love, you'll never work a day in your life."

Easier said than done.

If you're at the start of your career, perhaps it's a bit simpler to find and follow your passion. You don't have the clutter in your head and complexity of lifestyle that keeps you stuck in the murky world of decisions already made and paths already forged.

These workforce newbies still have a history, albeit shorter, that they're already contending with. Parental expectations, the painful reality of paying off student loans, or the pretentious chatter on sites like Reddit and Quora shouting you don't need a college education at all, only serve to create more noise that makes it hard to uncover where you want to go. There seems to be a huge rush to make permanent decisions right now.

It's hard to make life's decisions when everything should be possible, but the walls seem to close in quickly.

For the old-timers who have been around awhile, finding your passion can be hard. You've already invested so much in a particular career or vocation, making a change now might be seen as (a) stupid, (b) too hard, (c) embarrassing, (d) all of the above. The golden handcuffs – significant salary and benefits – are hard to give up. Add to this the impact on family members, an uncertainty of the success of a new opportunity, and you are immobilized from even *starting* to think about pursuing something different.

The day I was walking down the halls of the skyscraper overlooking the Chicago River will stand out forever in my mind. It was early in the morning, and I was the only one on the 29th floor. For my entire thirty-plus year career I liked to get to work early, so being there alone was a familiar feeling.

The outside offices had gorgeous views, and the high walls of outdated cubes created a cavernous labyrinth from my office to the coffee room. As I made the trek, I became aware of a voice in my head. It had been there awhile, but I had been blocking it. *"I hate my job. I hate my job. I hate my job,"* was playing over and over. Whoa. Where was that coming from?

How long has it been there? What do I do? The voice *had* been there awhile.

At that moment I realized I had to do something. I knew I didn't love what I was doing. Despite the title, colleagues, clients, money, responsibility, and opportunity, maybe 20-40% of my energy was looking forward to what I was doing each day, while the other 60-80% felt like I was pushing a boulder up the hill. I knew that I didn't want to feel this way any longer. I wanted to flip that ratio so that the 60-80% was on my side and I was doing something I loved.

If I could be successful using my skills in a situation I wasn't passionate about, what would it be like to use them doing something I loved?

With coffee in hand, I went back to my desk ready to make a change. I wanted to enjoy my day even more than I was right now, day after day at my desk with my coffee in hand. It probably meant leaving the company and the industry I had invested in for twenty years. I had a right to be happy. Yup, it was time for a change, and I was committed to making it happen, however, I didn't know where to begin.

I started a two-year process of discernment to help set off on a new course for my life and career. This investigation path I took was not linear by any means. There were many stops, starts, iterations, loops, and do-overs. Fear and my inner critic (who I hadn't even formally met yet) were ever-present. I tapped into a whole lot of resources including conversations with my wife, family, friends, colleagues; reading books, articles, and blogs; prayer and reflection; sessions with a coach/counselor, and when looking back, I realize, a lot of patience and perseverance to keep pushing on.

My confidence was shaky at times throughout this process. Nonetheless, I had committed to find and do something that was more aligned with who I wanted to be and to be doing what I wanted to do.

> **When the headwinds are strong, and the undertow is bringing you down, believe there is something you are meant to do that keeps you moving forward.**

I knew I had passion and purpose for my life, but it was blurry. What those two years did was help me clarify my passion, and just as importantly, give me the confidence to embrace and pursue it.

UNCOVERING PASSION

Before you follow your passion, you have to figure out what it is. As Lewis Carroll says, "If you don't know where you're going, any road will get you there." You will wind up somewhere, but it's not necessarily where you want to be.

Just the very word, passion, is somewhat nebulous. The dictionary says it's an intense emotion or a compelling enthusiasm or desire for something. All true. I like to think of it as something that you love doing, you are good at it, and you know it makes a difference. If you're *not* doing it, something feels wrong. When you *are* doing it, you know you feel complete.

> **Identifying passion is more about uncovering it than discovering it. It is there. Clear out the layers of stuff that keeps it hidden.**

We are not as aspirational as we can be. We don't dream wildly. We shut down hopes and wishes too soon.

Remember when you were a kid and you had free-flowing ideas of what you wanted to be when you grow up? It's a cliché, but kids wanted to be astronauts, doctors, firemen, cowboys, nurses, president, explorers, artists, and more. Naturally, people still pursue this quest for these occupations and accomplish the search, but so many people don't. Or they wind up in positions not out of a conscious dream, but an incremental series of decisions that bring them to a point they may or may not want to be at any longer.

I was working with a client who was extremely frustrated with his job, and it was spilling over into his personal life. If he rode the L, Douglas would have been one of those listless individuals coming downtown with barely an ounce of enthusiasm. Douglas was an experienced, talented, passionate individual who had clearly been deflated. He was in a very dark place. It was difficult, knowing his background and success, to see him exuding hopelessness and negativity.

I often ask the "genie in the bottle" question that challenges you to aspire, to think about what you want your life to look like. For a moment suspend the realities of money, geography, and relationships. The genie has given you three wishes, and you must use them to imagine yourself in three different scenarios.

When I asked Douglas this question, one of his aspirations was to buy a sailboat and sail around the world. I *love* asking questions I don't know the answer to, and I *never* judge an answer or tell someone that they can't do something. Have there been people who have chucked it all, bought the boat, and spent the rest of their life at sea? Absolutely. Who's to say this guy couldn't pursue that path as well? Certainly not me.

What I did ask was, "Why?" What is it about that vision that makes it so appealing?

First, he said it was freedom. The freedom to be on the water, and to be able to wake up every morning and decide where he wanted to go. He wasn't going to go fast or far, but it didn't matter. He could literally chart his own course every day.

"What else?" I asked.

"I love working the equipment on the boat that makes it all happen," he replied. "I can control what happens by working the tiller, the sails, and all the lines to make it go where I want it to go."

The conversation went on, and I was already learning so much. First of all, his energy shifted. When we shift from the inward "woe is me" or focus on all that is not right with us, we literally activate a different part of our brain that helps us see possibilities. If he continued to stay in that place of negativity and frustration complaining about his job, he could not have come up with ways to get unstuck. Physically and chemically we have so much cortisol flowing through our systems at times like that, and there is no way to look for other ways out. When we shift our energy to that place of aspirational thinking, positivity, and opportunity, the executive function of our brain is activated, and new solutions present themselves.

Secondly, Douglas's description of what an alternative life might look like revealed several insights into things he was passionate about that were not necessarily being honored in his life at that moment. Our dreams are built on things we love or are good at. Sometimes we cannot see the connections ourselves.

After a little more talk about sailing, I moved the question back to the here and now, "So, what's going on at work?"

His new boss had started six months earlier. The dynamic of his team's work had shifted, and the boss was a micromanager. There were long days of meetings and what he considered senseless discussion around tactics that were not advancing their goals as rapidly as in the past. This slowdown in productivity and progress was compounded because of the new boss' need to be involved in every aspect of the work. Unnecessarily so, in my client's view, because he knew what he was doing and didn't need her to challenge or redirect his work every step of the way.

Two of the things we learned were important to him in the sailboat conversation were now missing from his work life.

He had lost freedom at work. In the past, he could lead the team by confidently planning the direction the projects would take. He was a creative, seasoned veteran and loved the smell of success by helping the team move on a course to reach their goals. He didn't have the freedom to wake up every day and plan the course because the new structure had imposed constraints on his creativity to solve the problems and keep moving ahead.

He had also lost control. He loved working the parts of the boat to get where he needed to go. Of course, some challenges would come up, but he was able to be in charge to make the course corrections on his own. In the new world at work, he needed approval from his boss at every turn, and that slowed and impacted his skills and the vision he knew he possessed.

With those gone due to restructuring and a new management style, Douglas was no longer happy and fulfilled, nor passionate about what he was doing. The next steps were to help re-evaluate his current situation and decide to make it work where he was, or to move on to something else.

Uncovering your passion helps create the North Star that helps keep you moving forward.

When we are engaged positively and energetically with others and our world, oxytocin, dopamine, and other neurotransmitters are released and that activates the prefrontal cortex that allows us to be creative and create new experiences for ourselves. Alternatively, criticism and fear cause cortisol to be streamed throughout our bodies, causing our primitive brain to be activated and the only responses we can have are those of fight, flight, freeze, or appease.[1]

This same shutdown can happen when you want to dream about what you might do next and instead, are bombarded by the thoughts and statements we hear (or create ourselves) that shut down the ability to aspire. "You can't make money being an artist." "Why spend all that time and money on

---

[1] Judith E. Glaser, *Conversational Intelligence: How Great Leaders Build Trust and Get Extraordinary Results.* (New York: Bibliomotion, 2014). Chapter 2.

college, Bill Gates never finished." "It's too risky to start your own company, keep your day job."

All well intentioned, yet the comments repress our ability to aspire to something more significant for ourselves that uncovering our passion would allow us to do.

What's even more frightening is when we hear these words from someone in authority, they carry even more weight and are harder to dislodge from our memory.[2] Don't worry, by looking back and better understanding or reframing those comments, you can be free from the impediment, and begin to open up that ability to dream.

Douglas had found himself in a place of distrust and negativity. Some of it was externally created, and much of it was internal. He had choices to make as to how to handle his new reality. He could quit. He could suck it up and be miserable. He could choose to complain about the new boss with his co-workers and create an atmosphere of even more negativity. He could try to develop a different sort of relationship with his new boss to understand why she was leading in this way, and whether there were alternative ways of working together. Using this new lens of his passion and what was important to him, *he* had the opportunity to make decisions to realign and determine how he wanted to move forward.

Douglas stayed a bit longer with the new boss and then set on an intentional search for a new role. Through coaching, he had gained clarity around his passion for the things that he liked to do and was good at. He also had a better read on his values and the things that kept him grounded and inspired to work hard to be successful. His new role took him to that place where he had more control and could deliver the impact that was so important to his sense of purpose and fulfillment.

Once you have an idea of what really drives you, it's then time then to overcome what's holding you back from genuinely incorporating your passion into your life's plan. Do you have the skills to achieve it? Can it be grabbed hold of right

---

[2] Benchmark Communications, Inc. The GreatingWE® Institute. Conversational Intelligence® for Coaches. *Amygdala Threat Responses.* Reprint. 2017.

now, or is it the start of the process? Is it aligned with other values in your life? How do your strengths support the pursuit and achievement of this passion? What would it be like to live in a place where you're doing what you love?

If you're successful doing work you don't fully love, what could you do if you focused all your energy on something you're genuinely passionate about?!

Having the confidence to dig deep and ask yourself those questions help get you on the path to look hard at what you're doing and why, and start to move you towards that place of happiness, success, and fulfillment.

Through my discovery, my passion began to emerge very clearly. I honestly liked helping people, and I also wanted to see people succeed. This orientation shouldn't be surprising as I grew up in a "family of preachers and teachers." Many of my family members across generations made their life's work helping and serving others through ministry and education, and growing up I was surely planning on one of those paths.

When I was clear what motivated me during my corporate career, it also became apparent what I didn't like, and frankly things I just wasn't very good at. It helped narrow the consideration set of choices that lie ahead. I could focus on fewer options and throw my energy against those.

It was time to reconnect with those early passions, and understand why they were important to me, and what that might look like some 40+ years later. For me, I chose the path of figuring out how coaching could help me align more fully with my passion.

TAKING ACTION

Start peeling off the layers of fear and doubt that have buried your passion by engaging in the two exercises that follow.

This is an exercise to help you reconnect with that 7-year-old child who was not yet fully encumbered by the harsh realities of life and was willing to dream. Read through this yourself in advance, or ideally have another person read the script and guide you through the exercise.

Take your time.
This exercise can take up to 15 minutes.
Use the time to relax and open your mind.

Sit up with your feet on the floor. Hands on your lap. Take a deep breath. Gently close your eyes. Take 3 more deep breaths - in through your nose, out through your mouth. Make them deep. If people were sitting around you, they should be able to hear your breaths. Return to normal breathing. Feel your hands and their weight in your lap. Feel your torso pressing down on the seat of your chair. Feel your feet and their weight on the floor. Feel the pressure on the floor going down to the center of the earth. Now come back up and listen to your breathing. Now go back in time. Go back to the earliest memory you can recall. You were very young. Start thinking about fun things. Family, friends, games, toys, holidays, good times. Now slowly move ahead in time - Kindergarten or an early grade. Now stop there. Think about a teacher or an event that was memorable to really anchor you in that time. Now think about what you were doing at that time. Think about the games you would play. Make believe games. People you would pretend to be. Imaginary friends. The activities you did. Which ones are particularly memorable? Why? What did it feel like when you were playing in this way? **Now,** still at that time, think about what you wanted to be when you grew up. What did you want to do? Who did you want to be like? What role did you see yourself playing? What did it feel like to imagine yourself doing that? Now slowly be aware again of your breathing. Slowly open your eyes.

➢ Now write down first, what were the games and activities you were playing that you loved.
➢ Second, write down what you thought you would like to be when you were a grown up.
➢ What did you imagine that job would entail? Why did you want to do it? Why would you be good at it?
➢ If you're doing that job now, great! If not, why not? What would that job offer you that you're not getting right now?
➢ What elements of that job are you glad you're not doing today? What aspects of that job do you wish you had today? Can you find them?

The second is the "genie in the bottle" question that helps you dream unfettered, and the magic happens not in the what you want to do, but the why.

Imagine you are walking along the shore. It's a peaceful, regular day. You see a magic bottle in the sand. You pick it up and start rubbing it. The genie emerges and says you've been granted three wishes (No, you can't ask for more wishes!). "If you could be doing anything, anywhere, what would it be?" You can ask for three different scenarios of the perfect life for you. The exciting part is you do not have to feel constrained by the current realities that often get in our way. Don't limit your dreaming by relationships, money, location, or anything else. Those can all be part of your dream. Imagine three perfect lives!

➢ For each of the three scenarios, describe what the life looks like: what are you doing, who are you with, where is it located, how do you *feel* in that place?

➢ Look deeply at each of the elements of where you are, what you are doing, and who you are with, and ask yourself:

> ➢ Why does each of those elements seem so important?
> ➢ Where am I finding those in my life right now?
> ➢ Where are they missing?
> ➢ When have I had them in the past? Or, have I never experienced it?
> ➢ What would life *really* be like if I was experiencing life in this way?

Chapter 3

The Confidence to Connect

To get to the next level of greatness depends
... on the quality of the conversations.
Everything happens through conversations!
Judith E. Glaser

Shut up and Listen.
Tim Ressmeyer

"You were really listening to me."
At the start of my coaching career, that statement took me by surprise, as a client said it to me, and then another client reiterated that same statement. Because of the frequency that I was hearing *"you were really listening to me,"* it was obvious that is was a significant problem. It makes me sad to think people are so regularly *not* listened to. It also highlights the value of coaching – a place people can be heard – and even more importantly, an opportunity to help people learn to listen and to ultimately connect with each other more successfully.

When people connect, amazing things can happen. Trust is established, relationships are strengthened, and problems can be solved. Without listening, you cannot connect. Without connecting, you cannot effectively create experiences that bring about results, whether in your personal or professional life. People have a primal need to connect with others.

Everything changes when someone feels they are being heard. Listening is a skill that you want to practice and perfect.

Linda was a new client who worked for a major financial services company and was frustrated that her book of business wasn't growing as aggressively as she would like. Even more painful was the fact a couple of clients had left her recently, and she was afraid the trend would continue. She wanted a coach to help her get back on track through goal setting and accountability to get new clients and to stop the losses. She knew the steps and processes of sales – she had been doing this a long time – and she realized she would benefit from coaching to make sure the plan was given the greatest chance of success.

It was the start of a new year, so it made sense to be making such commitments.

One of our early sessions focused on strengths and aspirations. We were identifying how Linda could capitalize on what she was doing successfully, and map those wins to the goals she was setting for the year. Intuitive listening includes not only hearing the words but listening to what isn't being said. I asked curious questions that showed I cared and wanted to know more than just the simple metrics she wanted to set. A place of trust had been established between us. We connected.

Linda casually mentioned the value of independence and interest in perhaps someday running her own business and move away from her current mega company. It was shared as a bit of a pipe dream and something to consider at some point in the future. A discernable shift in her energy took place as she talked about this. I pointed this out to her, and we briefly discussed what that independence might look like. We resumed our focus on goal setting for the new year.

I did not realize at the time I called out her shift in energy, the profound impact it had on her. She later shared with me that when I told her I saw that shift; she knew she had to make it happen. Because of our connection, something amazing was created.

Our subsequent sessions started to include this element of exploring the genuine possibility of her starting her own company. We patiently worked both streams of building her current business while looking longer term.

The connection that was created through sharing, listening, trusting and exploring brought to the surface something so vital to her that it changed her life. Her confidence soared, and slightly more than 12 months later we were toasting the successful launch of her own company.

Listening in this way helps you connect with others, and the impact is tremendous. We all know when someone is only half listening. And that's not very satisfying. We know people who listen and then just try to contradict what was said, and you feel drained from having always to be defensive or acquiesce. When you truly listen you are looking at the person in the eye, putting thoughts of judgment out of your own head, and really listening. That is the foundation for connection. That is the start of surprising outcomes.

When you listen to connect – and not just to hear – you can unleash the unlimited capacity of both of your minds.

You need confidence to really listen. Typically, we think of confidence regarding speaking clearly and with impact. Seeing leaders and motivational speakers at the podium inspiring the masses through confidence of body, voice, and words is powerful. We consider these people to be confident. Very true.

There is the recipient, however, who also must have confidence. They must be able to hear the message and be willing to take it or leave it or to assimilate it into their own framework of thought. Not everyone delivers feedback or instruction in a way that makes it easy for the listener to hear. Our history and learned biases influence our ability to listen effectively when a spouse, boss, colleague, or client brings up something we may not want to hear.

When we hear someone say something, we judge the delivery as well as the content. In other words, are they saying it in a way that I *can* hear and accept it? Are they saying something I want to know or can agree with? Neuroscience research tells us that within .07 seconds of meeting someone our primitive brain decides whether they are friend or foe, and in .1 seconds our executive brain is processing the words being spoken.[3] That means the body language and voice tone impact us before we understand the words. It all happens quickly, and both the style of delivery and content are affecting our ability to connect.

Carol was a successful, no-nonsense kind of leader responsible for an extensive organization with hundreds of employees. In a coaching session, she described her challenges with a highly valued subordinate, Sherry. Her senior leadership role required that Carol give direction and feedback all the time. Because of her position, Carol's decisions had to be made efficiently. It was Carol's style of leadership to be clear and decisive. Sherry, unfortunately, tended to shut down during some exchanges, and Carol couldn't understand why. The feedback and direction she gave were in the regular course of business, and rarely was it of significant magnitude to elicit the response, she felt, from Sherry.

This communication impasse was brought up at one of their one-on-one meetings. Sherry shared that she felt personally attacked at those times, and ultimately her feelings had been hurt. Carol's response was, "This is business, leave your feelings at the door." Both sides had reason to be dissatisfied

---

[3] Judith E. Glaser, *Conversational Intelligence* (New York: Bibliomotion, 2014), 76.

with this pattern. Carol thought she was efficient; Sherry thought she was being attacked.

This dynamic was working for neither. You can justify Carol's approach, "I don't have time to dance around your feelings. Stuff has to get done. Stop being a snowflake." Carol had become reluctant to give hard feedback because she sees Sherry withdraw and later has to have all this talk about feelings. This. Isn't. Working.

Sherry's perspective was different. She was thinking, "Carol's not even giving me the chance to provide my perspective. She's just barking commands without acknowledging my situation and what else is going on."

Both can alter their approach to have a more impactful exchange, *and* create a foundation for better connection moving forward.

Repeated negative exchanges create a pattern that serves neither participant, and damages relationships and productivity.

There's a third party in such an exchange. In addition to the boss and the subordinate, there is the relationship, the connection. When you focus on something that transcends the two people in the dialogue, each participant c*annot* make it all about themselves.

When the connecting isn't working, and you're going into a challenging conversation, each person can ask themselves, "What is our bigger purpose in this conversation?" The answer might be, "To create an environment to quickly solve problems where each of us can come away feeling respected and confident we know what's expected."

Carol can dial up her emotional intelligence by thinking about the *outcome* she wants from this exchange, "Do I *only* want to get that next task done or do I *also* want to foster a relationship with this valued employee beyond this instance?" Ego is coming into play here as the boss feels she has the right to insist something gets done. And she is right, to a point. The boss would benefit, however, from creating an atmosphere where she can deliver feedback, be open to appropriate input, and move along quickly to other tasks.

Because the dynamic is not working for Sherry, she too can take a different perspective. Currently she is making it all about herself. Whatever has created this filter that tells her to take feedback personally is not working for her. She would benefit from reframing the situation. That initial thought that she is being attacked or invalidated is not true in this situation. Changing that thought when she hears the feedback to, "My boss has a more aggressive style than me, but she wants something done, and trusts me to do it" will have a different result. Or thinking, "I did mess that thing up, and I have to step up and do it over. She's not going to stop liking me over this," will help foster a healthy connection as opposed to one of distrust.

Sherry can focus on that higher order goal of developing a relationship with Carol based on a connection that transcends the interaction of the moment. Moving away from her fears and feelings of inadequacy, Sherry reminds herself that they *can* connect in a way to get things done. This allows her to focus on moving ahead.

When we are confident *listeners,* we help facilitate that connection that allows for an impactful exchange. We move away from our egos and biases to look at what is most important in this conversation. It takes confidence to step into discussions without all the armor of having to be right, or being afraid to engage, and in so doing you unleash intuition and the ability to create an outcome that allows both parties to move ahead.

The same can be true of making connections with groups. Leaders of large teams or organizations are frequently faced with conflict or misalignment, and the confidence to listen can facilitate growth and healing.

Think about going to a large sporting event. At times there is a clear message being shouted that seems to be coming from every person in the arena, "Let's Go Cubs!" is resonating from every seat at Wrigley Field; or so it seems. Sometimes, however, the message isn't as unanimous as it might seem. If the St. Louis Cardinals are in town, you can be assured there are a significant number of the 40,000 fans *not* cheering for the Cubs. It seems like a unified voice when in fact others are expressing a different viewpoint, or just not talking at all.

In leading groups, leaders tend to look at the group as a single entity. This can happen if the leader is new to the role and doesn't know the members, there is conflict in the team dynamic and cliques have formed, or the leader is in victim mode and feels *everyone* is against him or her.

Believing you are listening to a single message belies the truth in the situation. Mixed in with the raucous majority, or very vocal minority, are other voices that can be heard – if you listen. By learning to listen to these other voices, the leader can avoid the assumption that a) everyone is in agreement, and b) everyone is out to get me.

A very senior leader, Steve, was facing significant challenges with the topmost management levels in the division he led when he became a client. His leadership impacted thousands of individuals, and he was managing through significant financial challenges. The first tier he managed numbered 20 individual leaders, each with substantial accountability for many people in their area of the organization.

In working through the challenges, Steve tended to view this group of 20 as having a single mind that was in complete agreement all the time. Seeing them in this way is not an uncommon blind spot. Frequently I hear people speak of another group in their company (e.g. "marketing" or "operations") as being a 100% unified entity; as if they have a single brain. It is challenging to listen if you hear all of the voices as one, when in fact it is a collection of individuals.

A first step to change this dynamic was to start to look at the group members as individuals and to consider their unique wants, needs, and concerns, as well as ways they could contribute during this challenging time. When Steve dug into these 20 people with this mindset, there was indeed a great diversity of opinion as opposed to the perceived unanimity. The financial decisions that were going to be made would not impact each of the leaders in the same way. It was actually in their best interest to *not* be seen only as part of the larger group because blanket decisions might be made that ultimately impact them adversely.

By listening to the members as individuals, not only did they feel a more impactful connection with the leader, but they were also able to contribute to creating a shared vision for the organization to tackle the problems at hand. Each began to feel valued, and Steve was able to build trust and reach decisions more effectively.

The impact of confidence for both parties in a conversation is critical. When you are focused on connecting and not just getting the point across, you do things differently. You listen differently. You communicate differently. You strive to create a connection with the other person where both can be heard, and then amazing things happen.

TAKING ACTION

Connecting with others brings about remarkable change, and there are also many dimensions to it. The Connecting Wheel differs from the wheel presented in Chapter 1. This one allows you to think through these dimensions to help you understand the importance of each as you strive to connect better, as well as how satisfied you are currently with your performance with each dimension. When you recognize areas for improvement or change, that becomes your Action Plan for moving forward.

Look at the eight dimensions of the Connecting Wheel. These are eight ways that connecting with others can be enhanced or impeded.

8 Dimensions:

Listening – Focused attention to what the other person is saying

Intuition – Hearing more than just the words to understand more deeply what the other person is saying

Involved in Decisions – Being an active contributor to decisions that impact me

Communicating – Articulating my ideas

Collaborating – Working on opportunities or problems with others

Networking – Engaging with people beyond my closest circles

Relationships – Developing connections with people who are important to me

Trusting Others – Ability to believe those I interact with

IMPORTANCE - Score yourself on each of the dimensions. Number 1 is not at all important to me, and 10 is extremely important to me.

> How hard was it to score yourself?

> What surprised you about the results?
> What patterns do you see across the dimensions of what are or are not important?

SATISFACTION – Now look at each the dimensions again. This time score how *satisfied* you are currently with each of these dimensions. Number 1 is not at all satisfied, and number 10 is extremely satisfied.

> What surprised you about the results?
> Where do you see the biggest gaps?
> What patterns do you see?

ACTION PLAN – Now that you have seen both the importance and your satisfaction with each of the dimensions, you can set a plan for what you want to focus on. It's hard to tackle everything at once, so you might look for one or two areas to start working on right away. It may be where the biggest gaps are between Importance and Satisfaction, or it might be an area that's really been bugging you, and you know it's time to tackle it.

> Make a list of 2-3 dimensions you want to focus on.
> What would the value be if you improved the satisfaction by just a couple points?
> What would it take to improve your score?
> How do you want to do that and by when?

It can be very typical that these scores be different if you are thinking about your personal versus professional life. Feel free to complete the exercise separately for each. After doing that ask yourself why is different, and what can you learn from one part of your life to impact the other.

CONNECTING WHEEL

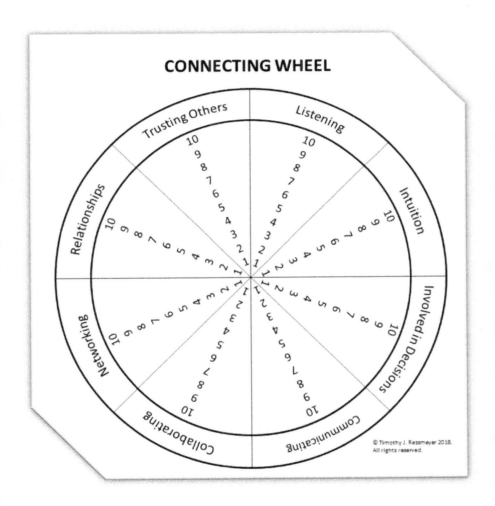

Chapter 4

The Confidence to Change: Transitions

Only I can change my life.
No one can do it for me.
Carol Burnett

Dude, Keep a Notebook
Anonymous Match.com member

We don't just face change;
we create change.
Tim Ressmeyer

Change shows up in all different ways. People respond to change differently. Sometimes change is a choice, and sometimes it is inflicted on us. When change happens, you have a choice how to react to it. Your confidence in handling change creates different outcomes. Change always presents opportunities. What do you want it to look like? How do you want to feel on the other side of the change? You decide.

Change happens in our personal and professional lives with the potential to create harmful adverse outcomes, or inspired new opportunities. You may have a new boss who was nothing like the last one who you really liked. You may become fearful you might not have your job for long. A new personal relationship may give you the hope and optimism that, "this is the one!" A spouse or someone important in your life may have an opportunity that shifts the plans you had made.

Sometimes change is in our control, and sometimes it isn't. We choose how we show up during change.

An executive coaching client, Gary, was a big player in a major corporation in New York City. Through mergers and other changes, he was unceremoniously cut from a role he didn't love, but it was full of perks and prestige. He was proud of the position. The money, the title, the travel, and the wining and dining were suddenly gone. He was devastated.

I was introduced to Gary by a mutual contact and began working with him while he was still trying to regain his equilibrium and figure out how to move on to what was next. It was almost a year since the termination. He was still angry and bitter, and the negativity was preventing him from moving forward. He had fallen far and was still in the deep hole of resentment and hopelessness. He was seeing a therapist to keep an eye on possible depression, and he had to move forward and figure out what was next.

We began with the baby steps of acknowledging how difficult this change was, as well as how difficult the past year had been. We started to revisit what had gotten him to the pinnacle of success in the past, and what he wanted to learn from that in the future. He looked into how the marketplace offered new opportunities and how he might adapt his skills to take advantage of it. And, we set up a relationship between the coach and the client steeped in accountability and forward motion.

Gary created a new career path for himself that he would never have imagined. He took the skills and experience he had in his prior roles and was able to reorient them in new ways to pursue a path he hadn't thought viable. It wasn't just the tactics of finding a new job that made this possible; it was the energy and confidence Gary had at his core to work through this new phase.

The stages he went through are not unlike the steps you go through in a personal relationship that ends and something new starts. You have a breakup, and you are experiencing all sorts of emotions, possibly positive and negative. Next, you start to figure you what you want to do next, and what you bring to the table. How do you want to show up in this new phase of my life? You then have to test the waters. Whether you're dating, doing a job search, or going through any other sort of change, you are interacting with others and exploring whether it's a good fit or not. Does it feel right? Am I the best expression of myself? Finally, you commit. I'm stepping into this new phase or role, and I'm going to make it work!

For me, using dating language is the clearest way to label – and remember – the four stages of transition and change: breakup, write the profile (ala online dating sites), dating, going exclusive.

Change and transitions are not always easy. You decide how you navigate the inevitable ups and downs of the process. Change can be executed with fear and anger, or confidence and opportunity.

Failing to embrace the four stages can lead to protracted pain and loathing, the dreaded rebound relationship/job, or the long-term sadness of never really finding what's right for you.

The Break-Up

Before you start something new, you have to have a breakup. For Gary having his job eliminated was the breakup, and it was painful. Getting promoted or intentionally ending a relationship is a break-up. Something has ended, and something new will occur. Even when you initiate the break-up, there is a new beginning.

When change is thrust upon you, there are tough times with emotions that legitimately are confusing and disorienting. Anger, hurt, fear, embarrassment, and sadness, are present. The feelings come at different times and stay for minutes, hours, days, weeks, or longer.

Awareness and acknowledgment that something has ended are vital. You had a role in it. So did whoever is on the other side of the decision. If it's really over, what happened has happened, and you cannot change it. You *were* in the relationship for a reason. You will have time to uncover all the "whys" and "what ifs" in the next phase. Don't try too hard to move on too soon. You can handle this! It is now part of your experience, and you will build on it moving forward.

Fear, desperation, and depression, are your biggest enemies. Don't give in, and don't move on without allowing yourself to feel.

There might be relief, joy, and excitement if you wanted the change. Being the initiator of the separation puts you in a different place than if you were the recipient, but it's a break up nonetheless. You might not be the victim, and this is still a time for reflection and an opportunity for growth to make sure your next move is as successful as possible.

Fully embracing this phase is essential to the long-term success of the transition. Giving yourself the time and space to be angry, cry, laugh, enjoy the freedom, or be inspired by the opportunity will set you up for success. This place is where trusted friends and family come in to help give you the space to feel. Ask for understanding and patience. They're most helpful to hold and support, and not to push you in places you're not yet ready to go.

The impulse to bash, judge, and vilify the "bad guy" in a break up is helpful to a point. These feelings may last days or weeks or longer, and that is alright, so long as you are looking back to learn, and over time make the shift away from them and on to what's next for you.

There comes the point where if your energy is still focused on them, they are in fact continuing to impact you negatively. *You* control your own energy. *You* decide how much power you are going to continue to yield to the other party. It's necessary to grieve and vent, and as you move towards the end of this phase, you're best served looking for what you learned, and not who's to blame.

Gary did not have anyone to guide him through the breakup, and it lasted a very long time. There does come a time when taking steps, even baby steps, get you out of this place of pain and into one of hopefulness and confidence.

Even though you might not be able to see it, you will come out of this. You will be OK.

Write Your Profile

Online dating was still relatively new and had just started to emerge as a respectable way to find lasting relationships in 2006 when I wrote my first Match.com profile. I was undergoing a significant change. I was coming out of a 22-year marriage that ended with a painful divorce. I was getting my feet on the ground and was ready to move on to a new phase of my life, and I had no idea what to expect or how to do it. I was first married at age 22, and now I'm dating again.

How do I write a dating profile? I figured out how to do it, and I met many wonderful people and came away with lots of great stories, some which will be told below, and most of which are best shared over a beer. I also learned a lot about how best to present myself in the midst of change.

Your dating profile is created so you are putting your best self forward to make a successful connection. It's a two-way street of articulating what you have to offer and what you are looking for while trusting there is someone on the other side who will resonate with this message, and a mutually beneficial relationship might result.

Your Match.com profile is not unlike creating your resume and cover letter when looking for a job. You are creating a description of yourself that includes a passionate articulation of what you bring to the table and what you are looking for in the next step of your professional journey. You are looking to create a meaningful connection. You are not begging for a job. You are not desperate. You are not going to twist yourself into something you're not to gain acceptance. You are learning to present yourself with confidence to the outside world.

You know you are giving your best when you are in a relationship/job where you are respected and valued. It is mutually beneficial because the other party is also able to contribute their best. It is the ultimate Win-Win.

Looking back to look forward is a great first step to move on into phase two. You are not starting out from scratch. You have a history whether it's 20 years or 60 years that has created you for this moment in time. You cannot go back and change a thing. Regrets are useless. "Woulda, coulda, shouldas" can keep you in a trap of either anger or a victim mentality that prevents you from seeing new opportunities and moving forward. You have survived those challenging times, and you're still standing. You will this time as well.

Gary had a particularly difficult time reaching this point. So much of his energy was still focused on blame against those who screwed him over or making excuses for what went wrong. He was not presenting a face to the outside world that would invite someone to want to take him on.

Unfortunately, we have been conditioned at times of uncertainty to look at what's wrong rather than what's right. Those things that didn't go as planned for us years ago are the first things that come to mind, rather than the substantially more "wins."

You can't start moving ahead if you are triggering the part of your brain that is looking to keep you safe. You are running forward into an exciting new phase, and you need your executive brain function in high gear to present yourself in the best possible way. You do have proof that you can do things well. Maybe some decisions didn't work out as planned, and you would like a "do-over." That's ok, your accomplishments will carry you forward. Of course, there is more to learn, and maybe you will learn to pivot your expectations, but you've got this!

Your brain has stored all of these prior wins in sophisticated networks in your brain. Those are retrievable by creating the opportunity to reach in and find them. That becomes possible when you force yourself to identify what you're really good at and evaluate what you have done well in the past. When you look at this data with the eye of an analyst, you see patterns that help you clarify what you want next, and create that new path ahead.

Once you have done the reflection, it is time to put your message together in a compelling way that lets others know you're available and presents the best picture of you.

This self-awareness is hard work. It takes a lot of introspection, honesty, and confidence to look at your expectations in a way that creates a willingness to be ready for something new. Some of this can be done by yourself, and you can also enlist others to support this exciting exploration.

My eldest sister went through a difficult divorce very close to the time of mine. She was living in England, and I went to visit her. She knew that I was doing online dating, and sheepishly asked whether I thought it was something she should do and whether I could help her.

We sat down at her computer, and she started working on her profile. It was painful. She was reluctant to celebrate her wonderful qualities fully. She didn't truly recognize how those things she took for granted would be meaningful for someone else. She didn't know how to be bold in saying what she was looking for in a guy, because she didn't want to seem picky.

She didn't realize that you are at your best when you are in a relationship where the qualities of both parties work together to make both people successful. You can only do that if you are honest both about what you offer, and what you are looking for.

I sent her away from the computer so I could write her profile. I knew her well, and we had talked about what she wanted her future to look like as she moved into her mid-50s and on towards retirement.

She came back into her office, read what I had written and was floored. "This really is me?" Yup. I had only used her own words, passion, successes, and vision for the future. She was an English teacher, so after fixing some of my grammar and sentence structure, we took a few pictures of her in her garden, posted it on the UK Match.com equivalent and waited.

She had good responses, and after only a couple of weeks, one gentleman, in particular, stood out. They started dating and were married just a couple years later. They were a good fit and created an amazing relationship where they allowed each other to be their best selves.

She, with help, had presented a picture of herself that exuded clarity and confidence. It's not attractive to read profiles or resumes of people who come across as desperate, willing to please everyone, or so arrogant you could never imagine being in the same room with them.

It took Gary longer, but he ultimately was able to let go of the anger of his past. He took stock of the amazing skills he accumulated. He began to believe that this change could have a positive outcome. He crafted a message about himself that was now positive and forward-looking and no longer had the tone of fear and resentment.

The confidence of knowing what you bring to the table allows you to present yourself in the most impactful fashion.

Dating

The change you're driving is now moving into the real world. It's no longer hypothetical. You have to get out of your own way and confidently step into a new phase. You're dating.

It's all different when you're in the safety of your home looking at postings and reflecting on yourself and what will make you happy and successful, then when you actually have to put yourself out there and have to talk to people.

What will they think of me? Will anyone see me the way I see myself? I've had a complicated last relationship. What if that happens again? Will I ever be happy again? How will I talk about problems from the past? What should or shouldn't I say?

These are all legitimate thoughts and concerns. And, it's also exciting if you look past the fear to the opportunity. Wow! This one seems really, really great. What a fantastic opportunity this would be. If I wound up with this one, I would be so happy! I think I could make a difference here.

This next step is where you want to be. The hard work you did Phase 2 gives you the confidence to go out knowing you have something to offer. You start to realize you're not a fit for everyone, and that's ok. You *know* you have had success in the past, and you know you are at your best with someone who wants what you offer and you want what they can give you.

Despite the optimism of what might be, fear of rejection is front and center in this phase, and that's totally normal. You are proud of what you have accomplished, but not everyone is going to want you.

When Gary began talking with prospective companies, it was challenging. He was full of the judgment of how the industry had changed, and how the companies he thought he wanted to work for weren't interested. The ones who were considering him weren't offering the right compensation, and he felt, didn't value his credentials.

He had to decide was he going to remain angry, or figure out why it wasn't a good match.

Whenever experiencing change, lack of interest and not having early wins can be devastating and create even more barriers to moving forward. If there are no responses, or the ones being received aren't good fits, it's time to revisit how you are presenting yourself to those you are looking to attract. If the message you're communicating isn't working, adjust it. You are the same person with the same set of skills you have identified that you are excited to bring to the next relationship. The lack of connection might just be your marketing or personal branding.

My 20-year corporate career was primarily in consumer research and marketing for consumer packaged goods companies, and Procter and Gamble was one of my clients. Tide laundry detergent is one of their key brands. Tide brings a lot to the table. It takes out stains, it brightens whites, it has fabric softener, it smells great, it keeps colors bright, and it has a premium reputation. It's difficult to articulate all of those characteristics in a single advertisement or marketing campaign. Not all of those features are relevant to every consumer. Some preferences exist, and some people are looking for some things and not others.

As you are in transition, you cannot be all things to all people, and similarly, you have to make sure your message is reaching the right people, at the right time, in the right way.

If you're highlighting that you brighten whites and take out stains, but your target market doesn't care about those as much as it does being able to soften fabrics and smell great, you can adjust your message. There are others for whom the other features are important, and you can find them if you like. You can also use this as a time to decide what is it you *really* want to do in your next role.

You might be great at leading teams, and working with clients, developing new products, and you've done some strategy work. How do you want to spend your days? Where can you have the most significant impact? What areas do you want to emphasize so you can deliver as well as grow even stronger in that capacity?

Be honest with what you really offer, how it will contribute to your overall goals, and listen to the marketplace to find those who want what you provide and communicate with them in a way that they understand how you will be exceptional together.

You can't get the right message to the right people at the right time if you are not both speaking clearly and listening attentively.

Gary began to realize that what he offered was valuable, and it just wasn't going to be in familiar types of companies. He had to gain a new understanding that what he brought to the table was in fact extremely marketable. He began to listen more to uncover the needs of these young companies. Gary got out of his way to connect with people in a new way to look for new opportunities.

As with laundry detergent marketing, conversations during the dating/interviewing phase are two-way. Being clear and authentic with what you are offering is as vital as being wholly dialed into the person on the other side of the desk. Asking curious questions and listening for the responses without worrying about your next question helps you to focus on them so you can uncover if there is a connection worth pursuing.

A woman I had met online taught me this lesson, let's say, with great clarity. It was the second time we talked on the phone, and we were deciding whether to meet for a date. I wasn't entirely paying attention. Our conversation came to an abrupt halt when it became clear to her we were covering questions already asked and answered. Her reprimand was not necessarily harsh, but it was clear, "Dude, keep a notebook." She meant I should be taking notes, so I know who I'm talking with and what we have talked about in the past. I felt like an idiot. I was not keeping track of my interactions with her, so neither of us were able to discover if there was value in a relationship. Needless to say, that relationship did not move forward.

As an executive and hiring manager, candidates I've interviewed in the past who show an unwillingness to engage in the process of exploration through impactful conversation – both questioning and listening – tend not to be hired. Failure to participate in mutual understanding of wants and value delivered derails opportunities to move forward.

It's challenging to maintain confidence when things aren't moving at the speed you would like. Fear, frustration, or the impulse to settle during a protracted transition or search are normal. Frequently reviewing your strengths, the value you bring, and the small wins you are having help overcome these drifts toward negativity.

Know there is the right role out there; it's a matter of making the connection to make it happen.

Going Exclusive

Suddenly you find yourself in that place you couldn't even imagine at the time of the breakup. Someone out there really does want me!

It's an exciting and rewarding time, but a whole new set of fears can be emerging. Is this the right one? There are others in the pipeline; should I wait and see if one of those materializes? What if this turns out poorly like my last one; I thought that was going to last forever? Should I be asking for more and getting a better deal? What if I'm not as good as they think I am and I let them down?

These questions are normal and a natural part of going exclusive. There very well might be other opportunities that could work out for you. You can also spend an indefinite amount of time looking for the perfect arrangement when an amazing opportunity is right in front of you.

When you are clear on what you bring to the table, why you do what you do, and how you want to show up in the relationship, your side of the equation is set, and you can commit. If you are in that place of personal clarity and confidence, then you can see what the other side is offering, how authentic they are, whether what they offer will contribute to your success, and whether the commitment should be made.

Gary wound up taking a job with an innovative, cutting-edge startup. It was a dramatically smaller salary than he was used to, but he had come to realize there was significant upside. Gary knew he could make a difference, and within weeks, he was bringing leaders from the startup to meet his very valuable network of contacts in New York. He had also come to realize this change had helped him see where his industry was headed, and hanging onto his old expectations would never bring about the satisfaction he wanted. In his new company, he could learn new ways of doing things in real time. Gary was learning on the job, contributing, and creating something new. He realized this was a great place to be.

Gary had one obvious option, and based on the work we had done leading up to the decision, he overcame some distractions and took the job. In other situations, there is the fear that something better might come along. Or, you are choosing between several alternatives, and are reluctant to commit.

The need to make a choice you plan to stick with will show up in both your personal and professional life.

A client, Mark, confronted confidence to go exclusive as he went through the four phases of change, and ultimately had to make a choice.

Mark was let go from a very senior level position. I was one of several coaches he interviewed, and he brought me on to work with him during his transition. He did not see the termination coming, and even though there was change at the management level, he thought he would be safe. He wasn't. In the months following we worked together managing the transition, going through the job search, and setting the foundation for the time when job offers would arise.

He had been successful, had a well-maintained network, his family was supportive, and he was not in financial distress. These elements gave him the confidence to work through the search process with a high level of energy.

Nonetheless, along the way, there were stressors: seemingly strong leads that didn't materialize at all, conversations that started and then dragged on with little or no communication, trips to interview out of state that raised the question of relocation, positions he lost to the "other guy," and more.

Ultimately two companies seemed poised to make offers. They were both strong offers, but different in significant ways. Either probably would have worked, but Mark needed to cut the ties with one and commit to the other. He moved forward, landed the job, and moved ahead with this next career move.

He used the tools he had patiently developed to make the decision confidently.

We continued to work through his onboarding, and as he walked through the door, it was clear things were significantly messier than he was led to believe, and much of it landed on his desk. He discovered the time frame to turn around sales weren't as generous as he was led to believe. He was expected to make significant personnel terminations very quickly, including a member of the owner's family. Client attrition was much more a cause of revenue decline than lack of new business, so he had to quickly sure-up the quality of his existing account management team.

His impulse was to start to regret ever having taken the job. Buyer's remorse set in. He wondered if he could go back and get the position he had turned down. He took the circumstances very personally and expressed thoughts that he had been lied to during the hiring process, that he was being set up to fail, and the company was so messed up there was no hope. These were very natural feelings when your honeymoon doesn't last.

Through these early weeks and months, we continued to focus on how he could address these challenges by tapping into his confidence and his skills. Everything that he brought to the table and the reason he was hired were still valid. He avoided the slip into the negativity of feeling he was misled and blaming others for the problems, by seeing the challenging situation as an opportunity to bring about positive change, make an immediate impact, and help the company handle such transitions more effectively in the future.

He was able to work through this challenging time, and continues to serve in a top leadership role for the company.

The stories of Gary and Mark show that being intentional as you go through the phases of change, can set you up for success. The confidence to take each step at a time, and being aware of your reaction along the way, may not come naturally, but in the end, helps you make those reasoned decisions all the way through making the final choice.

TAKING ACTION

Change is amazing! Whether thrust upon you or done of your own making you decide how to show up and how to react to the new reality.

Being able to move forward with confidence can be challenging. Not everyone responds to change in the same way.

By acknowledging and leveraging the four stages suggested here, embracing change can be less difficult and more beneficial. Acknowledge a break up has happened and allow yourself to feel. Be very real about who and what you are and what you offer while being clear about what you want. Present yourself in a way that is authentic, excited, and impactful. When it's time to make a decision, do so with the confidence you will be moving ahead into an exciting new opportunity.

Each of these phases of transition are so exciting and important and can be delved into with greater depth. Getting yourself in a place of confidence knowing what tools you have available is a great start.

Below are two exercises to help get you started.

STRENGTHS

> List 60 strengths – from all aspects of your life. These can be as simple or sophisticated as you like (e.g., I'm good at taking care of my pets. I'm a great communicator. People ask me to solve problems, etc.)

> Yes, Sixty!
> After you've listed them, ask yourself these questions:

> > How do I feel now that I've made the list?
> > How hard was it to come up with 60?
> > What surprised me about the exercise?

> Look at the list and look for clusters or patterns in the strengths

> > What themes seem to emerge (e.g., interacting with people, fixing things, doing thing independently, etc.)
> > What do these patterns mean to you?
> > Which of these would you like to spend most of your time doing?

> Select the 5 (five) strengths that excite you the most.

> > For each strength, complete the sentence: Because I am _____ (fill in the strength), I am able to _____ (fill in the impact of that strength).
> > Write the five strengths on a card, and stick it to your computer or mirror, and use it as a reminder of what you bring to the table.

JOB HISTORY

What do my past jobs say about me? Let's be honest!

> Go back to your earliest jobs (mowing lawns, waiting tables, whatever!)
> Fill out the three columns for each job. Be as thoughtful and specific as you can be.

JOB	What I Liked	What I Disliked	What I Brought to the Table/Contribution

➢ Be very honest about what you did and didn't like and why.

➢ Celebrate the wins, and ask yourself why you were able to contribute?

➢ Look for and identify patterns: e.g., working alone, lots of people interaction, autonomy, creativity, outdoors, etc.

➢ This can help focus your search for the types of roles that will fit you best, and can also serve as a framework to ask questions during the networking and interview process.

➢ Eventually, add all of your jobs (and include different positions within each company.)

Chapter 5

The Confidence to Move Forward: Advancement

*We keep moving forward, opening new
doors, and doing new things,
because we're curious and curiosity keeps
leading us down new paths.*
Walt Disney

*Watch the traffic, not the people, or you just
might get run over.*
Tim Ressmeyer

I was about 13-years-old, and visiting a friend who lived in Manhattan. I was a Long Island kid and was not as experienced as Paul at navigating the craziness of the City. We were headed somewhere and came up to an intersection. I could see the light was changing to red, and I was following his lead and as he stepped off the curb. I assumed that meant we were going to make a move across the street despite the traffic signal. I was wrong. With his casual style and experience of having been raised on the Upper East Side, Paul had every intention of stopping in the street. I kept going and narrowly missed being flattened by a NYC cab. Mostly because of the fear that evoked as well as the embarrassment of not knowing better, that incident reserved a permanent spot in my memory.

Years later when that experience popped into my consciousness, I summed it up with the observation to "watch the traffic, not the people." By watching only those nearby, I was missing the bigger picture of what was happening further out, and it almost cost me my life.

When we listen only to those closest to us, we run the risk of missing opportunities.

This tendency is not unlike the pattern of creating our bubble that is reinforced by the information we can select, and people we choose to listen to and those we want to ignore. We can create our own reality that makes sense to us, but it might not be the best thing for us in the long term, and we might be missing significant factors just outside our bubble that could present exciting opportunities.

It's scary to push out the boundaries of your near-in experiences to not merely focus on the people or situations right in front of you. Past experiences and fear of the unknown all contribute to a reluctance to move forward. It takes confidence that is sometimes hard to come by to make that push or even to consider listening to other voices.

Seeing people move forward is perhaps the most gratifying part of being a coach. When clients are making the big life-shifts like a job change or retirement, and I see them looking at their options differently, it's powerful. More immediate challenges, such as managing conflict in a working relationship, are often discussed when in a coaching engagement. Bringing about change can happen quickly for the client by gaining a broader perspective that coaching delivers.

So often we are locked into a mindset of only looking at what is immediately around us, that we cannot see further ahead and what might be. We allow the fears, experiences, and voices to hold us back from pursuing options that might change our lives. How many times have you thrown an idea out there to change course, and have friends or family not daydream with you of how to make it happen, but instead focus on all the reasons it probably won't work. All too often we tend to look at what's wrong rather than what's right. The result is a diminished capacity to aspire or dream.

Having the confidence to look ahead and seize change is not easy. We talk ourselves into playing safe, and out of dreaming big. Or, when we do imagine big, we lack the resources and stamina to seize what might be.

Early in my coaching career, I had the opportunity to chat with my niece who was struggling with a career decision. Jessica had grown up on the East Coast and was currently living in the Midwest. She had done well in the ten years she'd been out of school. She'd held several different types of roles within her industry, but was ready to make a move, and wasn't quite sure what path to take. She wanted to move forward but the confidence and clarity to make a move was slowing her down.

It wasn't a formal coaching engagement, just a conversation, and I still wanted to utilize my newly-developing coaching skills. Being a family member, I could have easily slipped into the traps of giving advice, trying to figure out what was best for her, throw out a bunch of suggestions, shooting down ideas, thinking of her history and drawing judgements, calculating the impact on other family members, etc. These are all things we tend to do. I reminded myself of – and followed – three essential coaching skills and "listen, acknowledge and validate, and ask curious questions." I wasn't going to be wise old Uncle Tim dishing out sage advice!

Jessica knew she wanted to get back east, and had begun to uncover options out there. I asked her to describe the positions that had piqued her interest. I was cautious to push away my own biases and expectations so I could just listen to her words. By being present, I was able to let my intuition kick in so I could ask the curious questions. I was also mindful of her energy as she shared her perspective on the different roles.

The way she described one particular position was especially curious to me because she barely mentioned it at first, and dismissed it as "too big" and uttered the biggest red flag words of all, "they'd never hire someone like me."

"Why not?" I asked.

"The previous people who had that job had been there a long time and were all big shots in the industry. I don't have those credentials," was her reply.

My questions followed over the next hour or so, "Were they big shots when they started?" "What did they do that was effective and where are their gaps?" "What do you think they could be doing differently?"

As we talked, I could see and hear her energy shift. It got inspiring when she started talking about what she would bring to the table for the organization. I asked questions such as: "What could you contribute because you are younger?" "What skills have you learned over the past ten years that they do not have?" "How can you relate to segments of their market they have not been able to tap into?"

The confidence to move forward can be jump-started by asking questions about "why it can," and not "why it can't" work.

Jessica went back east, investigated and applied for the job, and several months later secured the position and became their very successful Executive Director.

She had the credentials and did the hard work through the process. What I offered was the chance for her to challenge some of the limiting beliefs and assumptions, and instead look at the role from why could it work, rather than why it couldn't. She was able to have the confidence to move forward when she freely recognized her strengths, and the value she could genuinely deliver became clear.

Had Jessica only listened to the familiar voices around her, she may never have pursued that role. Instead, she looked out more broadly – she looked into the traffic – and could see how she had something to offer and could navigate what appeared to be an impossible path.

To this day she admits she didn't even know she was being coached in our initial conversation!

Using Core Values to Help You Advance

In thinking of the traffic metaphor, knowing we want to move off the curb and navigate the fray is difficult when we don't know where to begin. If we're angry, frustrated, scared, or disillusioned, we're not at our best in making that next move forward. Uncovering core values can help to provide an intentional framework for understanding how what is most important to us can be our north star as we look ahead.

Whether conscious of them or not, we all have core values that serve as our compass as we go through life. Your values are drawn from a long list of possibilities that can include integrity, success, service, family, communication, happiness, honesty, friendship, professionalism, loyalty, connecting to others, and so many others. When we fail to honor our core values, our life is not in alignment, and we are likely to be unhappy. And often we don't even realize why.

It's difficult to advance when we aren't sure why we're not fulfilled where we are.

Whenever a new client says, "I hate my job, and I have to find a new one, please help me," that leads me to pursue a deeper understanding of their values. Typically, there is something out of alignment with their values, and that is making their life miserable. By uncovering what the root cause is – in light of their values – it becomes evident what needs to be addressed to realign and bring direction and purpose back into their lives.

A client, Karen, was struggling with where she was in both her personal life and her career. She had some recent difficulties with a partner, and the relationship she had with her family was also hitting some bumps. She had been doing well professionally but wasn't pleased with where she was headed.

From a list of about 60 values, I asked her to choose the ten that were most important to her, *as she defined them*. After selecting the top ten, I then asked her to choose the top five that were *the most* important. She struggled with this narrowing down as most clients do. We spent time looking at this winnowing process, and what it meant for her.

The most significant surprise was that the values that were always top of mind for her, accomplishment and achievement, didn't make the top five list. She always felt that taking the next step, making a lot of money, and having big titles were the markers of career success for her. Those were the values that were driving her. Even though she was successful and was making good money where she was, something was holding her back, and those external measures of success weren't helping give her clarity on her next move.

The five values that made her final list were: service, holistic, connected, communication, and fulfillment. We discussed these in detail. Among other insights, Karen realized that accomplishment and achievement were, in fact, by-products of her value of wanting to be of service to others. When she was engaged in roles where she was aligned with the service value, she was being recognized, making money, and motivated to continue to move forward.

As she considered making a job change, rather than looking at the money or the title of a new role, she focused on how her value of being of service, along with her other top values, could be honored. It created a different lens that she could use as she advanced in her career.

We also used the core values to help give direction to her personal relationships. Family was so important to Karen, and she was surprised that didn't make the top five values list either. Again, reflecting on this, she realized she is more confident – and not likely to feel judged by family members – when she is in fact engaged in service, looking at her life and career holistically, and not as separate buckets, and she is communicating honestly with her loved ones.

Rather than only focusing on her troubled personal and family relationships as a single problem that had to be fixed, she recognized that realigning on her core values across all dimensions of her life would improve her circumstances.

In the end, she left the role she was in and indeed moved forward confidently into a new position very conscious of why she was going ahead in that direction. Her attention to all of her core values helped her frame that decision, as well as understand how best to improve her family and personal relationship challenges in the process.

Being clear on your values – knowing why you do what you do – and having the confidence to embrace them, drives success personally and professionally.

Competence – You Have to Know Stuff to Move Ahead

I was working individually as well as collectively with the leadership team of a mid-size company. The coaching program was structured so I was able to develop personal coaching relationships with each member, as well as to work with them in small groups or as a whole team. I had the unique opportunity to understand the strengths and aspirations of each, as well as the overarching needs of the company.

One member of the group, Martin, was an extremely bright, capable leader who was highly valued. He had not yet officially earned a position as a top-tier leader or member of the C-Suite, and that was where he was headed, and there were obstacles.

Martin had vast industry experience. He was highly competent in specific technical applications, as well as other people-focused areas including marketing and customer relationship management. His unique blend of gifts and skills made him invaluable to the organization; however, he wasn't stepping up.

He had developed the reputation of being someone who points out problems to the leadership but has no intention of helping to remediate the situation. One of the senior leaders described him as the "guy who rolls the hand grenade into the room." He has called out a severe problem and is just going to sit back and watch it explode, expecting someone else to deal with it.

It was hard for the other leaders not to value the insights he brought because of his experience and perspective, but he was not doing himself any favors in moving to the next step professionally. His subject matter competence was evident, but the same degree of excellence was not showing up in his leadership behavior.

To advance, you not only have to be an expert in your subject area, but you also have to be a competent *leader* as well.

Working with Martin, it became clear he was playing it safe without really knowing it, and not realizing how it was impacting him personally and professionally.

He was frustrated, and shared with me he was actively looking for other jobs. He didn't feel like the rest of the company was moving in the direction he thought they should. He could see everything that was wrong, kept telling people, and nothing happened. He felt his skills could be used elsewhere where they would be better appreciated.

Two of his core values were trust and openness. At a gut level, he didn't believe he could trust the company to listen to him, and there wasn't the openness to ideas and change that were so obvious to him. It created uneasiness and lack of confidence that this should be the place for him to continue his career.

From the outside, Martin was not viewed as someone who is ready for the next level. The other leaders struggled with not being able to easily identify what was causing their hesitancy in seeing him in a more senior role. They *wanted* him to work out, but it just wasn't working.

In discussions with one of the senior leaders, it was evident they needed someone to take on responsibilities, so he could focus on the unique areas only he could do. Martin could step into that role of taking things off the plate of his boss because of his experience and skills. It would be a significant move for Martin professionally. Unfortunately, the "hand grenades" approach Martin was taking would not earn him serious consideration for that more senior role.

Martin could, in fact, step up and deliver more value. He needed to be aware that leaders don't just point to problems; they look for ways to address them.

If Martin was going to move into that higher tier of leadership, he had to develop leadership competencies and overcome his lack of confidence that he could do more than only work in his narrow domain, or only uncover problems across the company. He could, in fact, address those challenges, and be held accountable for success. Even if it wasn't smooth or perfect every time, his leadership wanted and needed him to step up.

Being a competent leader requires not only being an expert and having the knowledge. You are also served by having the confidence to share your knowledge and look for ways to have a broader impact. Leveraging that leadership mindset leads to more significant personal as well as professional success.

Martin stepped up his game and worked with leadership to create the role that would best serve him and the company, and he elected to stay with the company. He focused on developing a new set of leadership skills that would make him even more valuable. This intentional focus on improving his competencies served him personally because he was better aligned with his core values, and he was able to contribute even more to the company. The leaders in the company appreciated the difference it made to the overall culture of the company in having another leader whose skills were being more fully leveraged, and who was being groomed to advance into an even more impactful role.

Moving forward requires confidence to avoid staying in your bubble with limiting beliefs and fear of the unknown; being clear of your core values and how you can honor them where you are now or in what's next, and in understanding that to move forward you have to be competent. And, that competence extends beyond subject matter expertise and into the realm of leadership competencies to show others you're ready for the next level.

TAKING ACTION

Career advancement is contingent on being competent beyond subject matter expertise. The Competence Wheel allows you to think through eight key dimensions of competence to help you discover the importance of each as you strive to advance, as well as how satisfied you are currently with your performance with each dimension. When you recognize areas for improvement or change that will become your Action Plan for moving forward.

Look at the eight dimensions of the Competence Wheel. These are eight ways that developing competence can be enhanced or impeded if not addressed.

8 Dimensions:

Continuous Learning – Willing to learn as things change in my industry

Expert – Knowing a lot in specific domains so people know who to go to

Strategic – Able to see how what I do impacts and contributes to a bigger picture

Knowledge Sharing – Keeping others abreast of the things I know and discover

Idea Interaction – Able to see how ideas from different areas impact each other

Articulate Viewpoint – Able to state and support my point of view

Getting Buy-In – Being able to have others commit to my plans

Knowledge – Knowledge of content relevant to my organization and its purpose

IMPORTANCE - Score yourself on each of the dimensions. Number 1 is not at all important to me, and 10 is extremely important to me.

➢ How hard was it to score yourself?
➢ What surprised you about the results?
➢ What patterns do you see across the dimensions of what are or are not important?

SATISFACTION – Now look at each the dimensions again. This time score how *satisfied* you are currently with each of these dimensions. Number 1 is not at all satisfied, and number 10 is extremely satisfied.

➢ What surprised you about the results?
➢ Where do you see the biggest gaps?
➢ What patterns do you see?

ACTION PLAN – Now that you have seen both the importance and your satisfaction with each of the dimensions, you can set a plan for what you want to focus on. It's hard to tackle everything at once, so you might look for one or two areas to start working on right away. It may be where the biggest gaps are between Importance and Satisfaction, or it might be an area that's really been bugging you, and you know it's time to tackle it.

➢ Make a list of 2-3 dimensions you want to focus on.
➢ What would the value be if you improved the satisfaction by just a couple points?
➢ What would it take to improve my score?
➢ How do I want to do that and by when?

COMPETENCE WHEEL

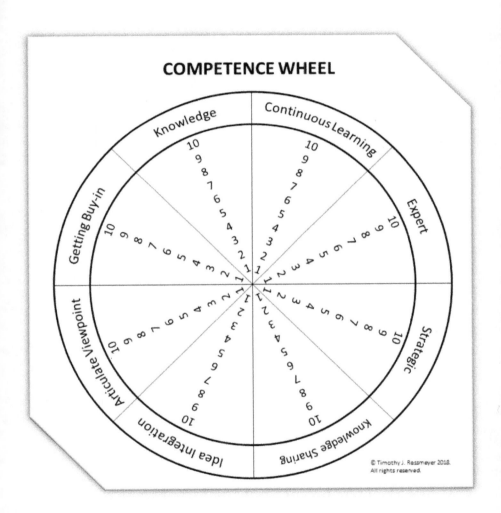

Chapter 6

The Confidence to Trust: Relationships

What counts in making a happy relationship is not so much how compatible you are, but how you deal with incompatibility.
Daniel Goleman

Good people should know good people.
Tim Ressmeyer

The ability to create relationships follows our life stages. It's harder as we get older, yet it's critical to our personal fulfillment and professional success.

As a kid it's relatively easy to make friends ("Can Jimmy come out and play?"), in college it's straightforward as you have built in things in common and experiences (majors, classes, dorms, Greek life, etc.). As you get older, these built-in connections become less accessible. The demands of building careers and creating families lead to more isolation and less time to be social. Societal fears about keeping our children safe make us less engaged. Social media channels that have redefined what relationships can be, and workplaces that demand more and more of our time – our most precious resource – limit connections.

All these factors hinder an ability to create new or meaningful relationships. It's a little creepy to go next door and ask if Jimmy can come out and play when you're 50-years-old!

In the workplace developing impactful personal relationships takes careful navigation of the culture as well as politics within an organization. Most corporations have policies that put guardrails around socializing with co-workers. Whether 'ok' by the book or not, developing relationships at work are natural. When you're spending most of your waking hours in the office, it's natural to form relationships with colleagues. It's the most accessible place to meet people, you know something about them, and there are built in commonalities. This can fill that void and difficulty of making relationships elsewhere.

Developing professional relationships at work requires an additional layer of confidence and clarity to help you find career success. As an employee, being conscious of how you interact up, down, and to the side drives effective relationships. How do you make sure your boss and those above are seeing you in the way that most effectively helps you do your job? How do you treat those that report to you – or other support personnel in an organization – to foster relationships that are aligned with your values? Are you addressing your colleagues and peers in a way that supports your ability to create a culture that drives success for all of you?

I'm not a fan of the language of "managing up," or down, or to the side (peers) in organizations. That tends to make it all about you and puts a lot of pressure for you to do everything right, and it can also feel manipulative. Rather, you are always creating *relationships* in all directions. How do you want these relationships to look? There is value to you and the other person to have a connection based on "We," and not "I."

When navigating interactions with colleagues, it's not just about the task at hand. There is another person involved with you, and you are in fact creating a relationship. When you connect with them and focus on what shared success looks like, you can create amazing outcomes.

Successful relationships are based on trust, and it takes confidence on your part to create a place of trust with those around you.

Scott became a client of mine about a year after he joined the senior leadership team of an organization as a Division President. He had good prior experience that qualified him for the role, and it was still a significant step up for the amount of responsibility, visibility, and impact. He had over 20 leaders to oversee who in turn managed over 300 full and part-time employees. His boss reported to the CEO of the company. There were not many levels above him.

He came into the role and struggled with the isolation that comes at the top of the workplace pyramid. In previous positions, he had peers to bounce ideas off of and from whom to learn. New to the organization he wasn't sure about agendas and who he could trust. He had moved his wife and children across the country for this role, and although supportive, he was reluctant to share all his fears with her.

Confidently learning to create relationships above, below, and to the side is essential for success.

Relationships Above

One of my favorite reminders to employees is that your number one job is to make your boss successful. That's it. When you understand what it is that helps your boss look good, get her bonus, and meet her goals, you shape your work to help bring about that success.

Scott had a tough boss when he came into his new role. The boss was not clear on articulating his own goals, allowed lower level people to go around Scott when problems arose and was unable to help clarify or implement the CEO's higher level vision.

Through the coaching and leadership development work we did together, Scott began to work intentionally to develop a relationship despite the apparent lack of willingness of his boss to communicate effectively and work together. Scott learned to avoid blaming himself for the dysfunction and instead worked to find small wins where progress could be made. He started to look at every conversation as an opportunity and managed his expectations as to what he could expect from his boss. Through these areas of focus, he made significant progress, and although frustrating much of the time, he learned to avoid feeling like a victim or being angry at the situation and continued to work to create a productive working relationship so they could both achieve their goals.

Although slow, there was progress, and Scott had developed a new style of working with leaders above him.

When the boss decided to leave his role, Scott was provided the unique opportunity to develop a relationship with his new boss that would hopefully be more productive than the last. From first appearances, the new boss seemed more willing to engage, but she was coming into a high profile position and would encounter the same lack of support that Scott had experienced. Scott drew parallels to his own experience of being new and isolated in the organization and worked to develop a relationship with his boss that would provide her with more of the connection and support Scott had been denied.

Tapping into his confidence, Scott took the initiative in creating a working relationship. He didn't sit back and wait and see what the new boss would be like. Neither did he follow the impulse to drop all the problems on her desk expecting her to fix things for him. Instead, he built a relationship founded on trust where they were able to have healthy discussions, navigate landmines, challenge each other where necessary, and work towards their mutual goals and achieve success.

The effective relationship Scott created above him was especially helpful when external events generated a significant amount of upheaval in the company during the first year of his new boss's tenure. In crisis mode, and under attack, he needed his boss to help him navigate the severe issues that arose. Through this time, Scott also recognized his boss's success was tied to the way the problematic circumstances were handled. Scott continued to have a broader view of the situation, avoided making it all about him, and together they were able to mitigate the problems successfully.

At the same time, his boss was able to communicate upstream to the CEO that despite the problems, there was a plan, they were working together, and they had the CEO's interests in mind as well. This trust at the next level above helped the CEO give support to Scott and his boss.

Developing relationships with those above you are based on trust and are best created before the crisis erupts.

The relationship Scott created with his boss from the start of their relationship was based on a confidence that Scott had something to offer, was not afraid to ask for help where he needed it, and kept his eye on what was necessary to his boss's success. This intentionality created an impactful working relationship which helped them efficiently work through challenging situations.

Relationships Below

My parents raised me to never look at anyone as being more or less valued or respected than anyone else. A server should not be treated differently than the restaurateur. The CEO should be shown the same level of respect as a member of the janitorial staff, and the store clerk should be granted the same courtesy you would give to the owner.

I grew up with these values, and they were reinforced on my first day of graduate school. I had a teaching assistantship, and my advisor gave the advice to be sure to get to know the administrative support staff in our department and to treat them with the same respect you give to the Chair of the department. Part of it was utilitarian in that he was recommending you "get on their good side" so you could get them to do things for you. Failing to do so could make life harder for you.

I took his guidance to heart, and even though it was part of my upbringing to treat everyone with respect, the solid relationship I built with that administrative assistant in my grad school department did have material benefits. I was coming down to the wire with getting my final master's paper completed by the deadline. Home computers and word processors were still not around, so typewriters were the only method available to produce the paper. I was a decent typist, but not fast or accurate enough for what was needed. I asked Irene, and she was more than glad to finish the typing for me so I could meet the deadline! I'm so happy my advisor reminded me of the sage advice to build relationships with everyone.

Creating a relationship with people at levels of an organization that fall below yours not only is the decent thing to do, but it also makes for greater career success. People who follow the model of aggressor or bully leadership are not as impactful as they might be. They exhaust themselves and don't draw out the best in others.

When advising on politics and leadership, my father always said to look at the people leaders surround themselves with because it is a reflection of the type of person they are. Are they looking for "yes men" or are they surrounding themselves with the best and the brightest; people who can support as well as challenge? Are they people who can introduce different perspectives into the mix to come up with the best solutions? Are they from various parts of an organization and not just the "inner circle?"

One of my business mantras for years has been "I'm never the smartest person in the room." As a leader, I always know there are people around me who know more about relevant topics than I do.

Leading a consumer insights team, I knew I had critical strengths to make us successful, and I also knew I needed my team members to take hold of things I was not as good at. I was good at using our research findings to address the business issues we were trying to solve, and fortunately, I had better analysts than me to build the models and crunch the numbers. I was always willing to learn from them, and together we could come up with amazing results. And, they were able to confidently move forward with their careers since they learned how and where to develop their impact in ways outside their core competencies.

It takes confidence to let those you manage also rise to the top.

Jennifer was new to her role as a manager of a team of six people when she hired me to work with her. She used to work as part of this same team, so when promoted, she had the unique situation of managing those who had been her peers the day before. That is never a comfortable situation, and being new to management it was a double whammy for her.

She knew she had to be intentional in developing relationships with this group from the start so that she could lead a successful team. A trap I see happen all too often is to look at a team or subordinates as a single entity. When you look at your team as "them" as opposed to unique individuals with skills, goals, and aspirations, you are minimizing what each can offer, and you create a rigid barrier when things aren't going well.

Jennifer was inclined to create standards across the team with the same sets of expectations for each member. They would all have the same basic tasks and success metrics. Those who weren't as competent in a particular area would be expected to improve. She thought it would make it easy to manage them that way if everyone was measured against the same benchmarks. As we dug into the reality of that assumption, she realized she did need different levels of production in different areas from each person. She spent the first weeks in one-on-one meetings understanding her team better, finding out their strengths and goals, and seeing how she really could create a competent team that played to their individual strengths to create an impactful group.

This approach took confidence on her part. She was willing to be flexible and to be able to steer away from a "one size fits all" style of management. She was developing a unique relationship with each team member where they felt valued and could see how they contribute to the overall success of the team. From a leadership standpoint, it appears to be more time consuming, and it is at the start. In the end having this unique understanding of those who operate below you helps enhance your effectiveness as a leader because you are drawing on a deeper pool of talent, increasing their level of commitment, and as a result, they are likely to be more productive and stay with you longer. You are better able to support them in their career development by tailoring training, mentoring, and leadership growth opportunities to their specific needs.

These are the underlying tenets of successful employee engagement.

Jennifer trusted and respected her team members, and they were able to do the same with her. There were difficult situations the first year, but Jennifer was able to navigate them and continue to strengthen the relationships. When there was conflict, she was able to be confident in the way she dealt with individual team members and could make hard decisions when necessary. Her team saw her as fair and respectful.

Relationships to the Side

Peer relationships in the workplace are challenging in different ways than either those above or below. In some ways, they're more comfortable if you're working with people in your same area of an organization and you have similar or mutual goals. However, there can still be personality conflicts or competition that impedes the creation of constructive relationships.

Where you are in the organization presents different dynamics as you develop relationships. If you and your business partner are running the company, that's a relationship to the side that is much different than if you are part of a larger leadership team. Similarly, a mid-level manager in a single department is developing relationships with peers that are different than if she is in a matrix organization where new challenges are introduced because you are representing diverse parts of the organization.

The two most important factors to help create relationships with peers are goal clarity and trust.

When working with peers, you have to know why you're both there.

Carl and Dennis were young entrepreneurs who had started their own company and were finding success very quickly. They were bright, creative, and very skillful. They were also both driven by the goal of building a very successful company.

As they started to achieve success, indications of difficulty in the relationship were beginning to concern both of the partners, and they reached out to me to work with them, not knowing where their company and relationship might be headed. A break-up was not out of the question.

Where they had always seemed to be on the same page, there was now confusion and mistrust and conflict was just around the corner. From the start, they had agreed to work as partners, and share the profits equally. Carl began to see this 50/50 split as being unfair. He felt he was putting in way more effort than Dennis, and it was working. The company was growing rapidly mostly because of his work, he believed. "Why should Dennis be getting the same return I am when I'm putting in so much more effort?"

Interestingly, Dennis was feeling an overwhelming pressure from Carl that he couldn't do anything right. Dennis was feeling judged and valued less. It was sadly becoming the type of experience he didn't necessarily want to be part of.

The coaching engagement I kicked off with them included individual coaching as well as business partners coaching (aka "couples coaching!") where I would meet with them together. It took a lot of confidence on *their* part to open themselves up in this way.

One of the most impactful aha's came when doing a personal goals and values exercise with each of them individually. They were each asked to write a personal mission statement that included their strengths, things they wanted to get out of life, the impact they wanted to have, and what their immediate steps would be to move towards these goals.

Both sets of goals were relatively similar. Being young, they wanted to create a lifestyle that would allow them to have families and comfortably support children, have free time for travel, and have their business be successful. Digging into what "successful" meant, they both wanted to be earning $1 million annually. The interesting difference was in the timeline. Carl wanted to hit that mark in five years, Dennis was happy to achieve $1 million "somewhere in the future." They both wanted the same thing, but there was a disconnect on timing. No wonder Carl saw Dennis as a slacker; he had a very aggressive goal in his head. Dennis was pleased with the growth of the company, knowing his goals would be met at some point in the future.

They *assumed* they were on the same page, but reality indicated something different.

We discussed this in our group sessions and worked to align their goals, clarify and appreciate what they each brought to the company, and to develop roles for each that would allow them to offer what they could contribute most to the success of the company. The result was a reinvigorated working relationship that resulted in much higher levels of personal fulfillment and professional success.

Relationships to the side do not always have to go "sideways."

In Carl and Dennis' situation, they were very closely connected to each other and the outcome. New complications are introduced when working with people from different parts of the organization who don't fall into the same reporting structure as you. Whether an actual "matrix organization" or just a need to work with people in different parts of the company there are different cultures, goals, and management styles in play. Understanding how relationships are formed within this framework helps you – and your colleagues – minimize failure and achieve success.

Danielle was a client who worked in product marketing for a large financial services company. She was at the VP level and managed a large team very successfully. Products were created, launched, and supported effectively. Her reviews were all very positive except for input from the sales organization within the company.

What Danielle was experiencing is part of an age-old conflict between sales and marketing. The same can be said when HR, finance, and other divisions are involved. If you have obstacles in dealing with other parts of an organization, and it's not slowing you down, stop complaining and get your job done. If, in fact, it is indeed a problem that is impeding your progress or your work, you will want to address it to bring about change. If it's broken now, and ignoring it or griping isn't helping, you'll need a different approach. In other words, own it.

Taking action from a position of positivity and confidence will impact results more so than operating from fear or anger.

Danielle was angry because the sales division was questioning her ability to deliver, and she was, therefore, getting lower scores in her review. There were three actions she employed to help overcome the obstacle.

Who is it?

The importance of not looking at a group as a single entity is an essential first step to help break down the obstacles and move forward. Danielle had the perception that the entire sales organization was critical of her performance. With further digging, it became evident that there were just a couple team members where there was a struggle. Even though it was not everyone, the fact that some team members were hurting her ratings meant it did have to be addressed.

When Danielle looked at it this way, it provided a new clarity and set her up for the next two steps. It did not seem as overwhelming when she just had to consider her relationship with a few members of the sales team. That, Danielle, could handle more easily. She also discovered that she *was* effectively working with many in the sales group. What could she learn from those relationships to help develop better ones where she was currently struggling?

What do they need?

The things that were causing the conflict were, in her mind, their fault. The sales team members were promising things to clients she felt were not reasonable, and she was therefore unable or unwilling to meet those demands. *"Sales should know better, and I shouldn't be blamed for not delivering against unreasonable expectations."* Danielle had to step away from the righteous indignation that she was being treated unfairly.

The approach taken was to look hard at what the individual in the sales organization needed from her to be successful. Understanding what they were motivated by and need to achieve shifted the focus from Danielle being defensive, to her being proactive and creative. It wasn't about her any longer; it was about them.

This confidence to figure out what they needed, what was broken, and how she could help them achieve that led to an entirely different conversation with the sales team.

How can I make it happen?

In Danielle's situation, she wanted to figure out what the win-win would be for her and the sales team. She wanted to be part of their success, and then presumably her ratings would improve as well.

After focusing on a clear understanding of what the sales team needed – and what they felt they were missing from her – she was able to initiate conversations with the contentious business partners. She held her ground on what she could or couldn't do, but together they were able to find ways to work together more effectively.

She was also able to bring her boss into the conversation. She had felt he wasn't supporting her enough, but in reality, she hadn't been able to articulate what was going on and how he could help her. He perceived her as just complaining about the scores which he really couldn't change. When he began to see the underlying problem, and Danielle was trying to rectify it, he was better able to step in to help.

Danielle had helped create a culture of trust because she was coming from a place of confidence that they could figure it out, that she did, in fact, want them to be successful, and there were steps they could all take.

Her relationship with the sales team improved, as did their assessment of her as a business partner.

Relationships, whether social or in business, are always evolving and changing. Sometimes we connect right away, and sometimes we don't.

Our circumstances and expectations impact the ability and need to develop meaningful relationships.

Stepping back and being clear and honest on what the purpose of any given relationship is, helps guide the direction of that relationship.

In the workplace, having the confidence to step in and create relationships with those above, below, and to the side of you helps you achieve the success you desire.

TAKING ACTION

- ➤ Make a list, by name, of all of those people in your business with whom you work.
- ➤ To start, select those who you feel are the most essential or key relationships.
- ➤ Assign each person in this list of your Key relationships into one of three buckets: Up, Down, To the Side, based on whether they are above, below or parallel to you in the organization's structure or hierarchy.
- ➤ For each of the Key Relationships answer the following questions:

  - ➤ Why is this relationship important?
  - ➤ What does success look like for the other person?
  - ➤ What motivates the other person?
  - ➤ What can I do to help us both achieve success?
  - ➤ What actions can I start to take now to create the relationship I want?

- ➤ From that last question, take those actions you can take, and turn it into an action plan which includes the first steps, and when you plan to start.

Note: You can do this exercise for all your relationships, and not only key ones by identifying those that are on the continuum of not very important to extremely important. It's helpful to classify relationships in this way to help establish how much effort you want to put into each one. You might tend to spend more time on less valuable relationships, and not enough on the key ones that you might be avoiding.

Chapter 7

The Confidence to Take Control of Your Life

When you lose the power to laugh,
you lose your power to think straight.
Jerome Lawrence, Inherit the Wind

You spend too much time at work
for it not to be fun.
Tim Ressmeyer

It was about 90 minutes before the scheduled start of a morning coaching session and I get an email from the client, *"I will be a few minutes late calling in this morning. There are some beer fest tickets that go on sale at 9am that always sell out very quickly."* ☺ I smiled, she scored the tickets, and we spent the first few minutes of the call talking about stouts, porters, and how best to pace yourself at a beer tasting.

I love it. I love knowing what my clients do to have fun and how it's incorporated it into their lives in order create the life they want. This is an example of having the confidence to take control of your life. This client knows what excites her in her life and she goes out and gets it. It's manifest in other parts of her life as well, and sometimes it's a struggle to set aside time for yourself – to take control – when things aren't going as well.

Taking control of your life requires the belief that you are worth it—an understanding of what excites you, and the confidence to make it happen.

When you start to take control of your life and not let work or other pressures dominate, you start to find the balance that helps make life fun. Being honest about what rejuvenates you helps create a view of the world that you are important, and deserve the fun things as well as the success you desire.

Not everyone is motivated by the same things! As I look at the choices my clients make, it truly reinforces the notion that you have to identify the activities that work best for you when you seek to round out your life. There are so many choices that are made: fitness classes, sailing lessons, marathon training, yoga retreat, art classes, sabbatical, hiking, travel, painting, reading, dating, not dating, volunteering, family outings, sky diving, biking, improv classes, beer making, and so many more.

Not to be a buzz kill, but before we can look at ways to bring fun and control into our lives, we have to examine the factors that take the fun away. Through this self-awareness, you are already on the way to create more fun. It takes confidence to look at yourself and admit the things holding you back, and confidence on the other side to bring about positive change.

We create our own stories; and they're often not true.

We are all the creation of everything that has happened to us up until this point in time. Every relationship, hardship, joy, loss, gain, job, heartache has created us and we can't change any of it. Regret doesn't serve you. We can learn from it. We can't change it. And, we have control to decide how we want to show up for what's next.

Unfortunately, there is a tendency to expect what happened in the past has to happen again. Whether we expect this outcome from our self or others, we "write a story" in our own head. A script if you will of how things will turn out. It's not always true! Too often these stories limit what we really can be. The past does not have to repeat itself. You don't have perfect information of what might happen. You can't control everything; you can control how you show up.

Learning to not make up stories frees us to experience what is in front of us, confidently make decisions, and take control of what's next.

These stories we write in our own minds tend to lean more towards the things that have gone wrong rather than reinforcing what has worked. Focusing on the problems creates a downward spiral of negativity that prevents us from finding solutions and outcomes.

We will look at things that have happened in the past, and assume that because they happened before, they will occur again. I frequently encounter people looking for a new job who have written off an entire company or industry because of one job interview that didn't go well. There might be a variety of reasons it didn't come through at that time, and it doesn't mean you cannot try again. Evaluate why it happened and ask the simple question, why does it have to happen that way again?

Other times we leap to conclusions we make without any real evidence. Imagine walking into a client meeting, and one of their team members looks at you and glances away without greeting you. Immediately you come to the conclusion that she doesn't like me and the meeting will therefore go poorly. How do you know that? Maybe she's thinking about something problematic that happened at home this morning. Maybe her phone buzzed and she was distracted. Be careful not to go down the path of negativity and making it all about you.

A good check on a tendency to leap to conclusions, is to run it through the "what's another way to look at it" or "what would my best friend say" test. Your boss challenged you on a decision and you can't believe what an idiot he is! Ask yourself; is there another way to look at what he said? How can I reframe his response to me so I have a more productive reaction? How would my best friend look at this?

We also carry with us beliefs about ourselves or the world that we have never experienced, but still believe to be true. "You can't successfully have a career and a family." "Unless you have an MBA from a top tier school you'll never be able to be successful." "You can never rise to the top with a Liberal Arts degree." Believing these viewpoints without questioning them can lead to decisions that don't play to your strengths, or allow you to control your own life.

A way to negate the impact of such unproven beliefs is to look for one instance when the belief is proven to be wrong. If others have proven it wrong, what would it take to follow that path, rather than give up without trying?

Our stories also come from our inner critic, or more popularly known as a Gremlin. It's that voice that tells you that you can't do something so why try. It can also stop you from taking risks so that you don't embarrass yourself. Most potently, your Gremlin brings up the thoughts of the imposter syndrome and suggests one day they will find out you really don't know what you're doing!

Getting rid of your Gremlin is impossible; it's been with you forever, and it will stay with you forever. What you can do is lessen the power of your Gremlin by naming it, reminding yourself of all the proof points you have that you are successful, and continually telling the inner critic to, "shut up!" and train yourself to not listen to that voice.

Unfortunately, there are chemical factors in place that exacerbate negative situations and help create this dark cloud of fear and frustration. When we encounter a situation – real or perceived – as being a threat, the cortisol that's released not only activates your amygdala to protect yourself from danger, but also triggers your limbic brain where all old experiences are stored. The result is a flood of memories of how you were hurt, embarrassed, or experienced failure. It's hard to counteract this if you're not intentionally training yourself to not focus, or take too seriously, the negative things that pop up. So many of these situations are not as problematic as we make them out to be, and we can train ourselves to be less pessimistic.

Outside Forces

We might write stories in our own head that hold us back, and there are also external factors that impact our ability to show up the way that we want and take control. These external influences can be very difficult to overcome. When we are aware of them, and recognize the impact they are having on us, we can cut ourselves some slack, or, take control back by addressing them head on.

Be aware of how physical, mental, environmental, social, spiritual, and emotional stressors impact your ability to be at the top of your game.

The impact of **physical** challenges on leaders can be the most difficult to deal with. That persistent pain from an injury or chronic ailment works its way into every part of our day. Think of having an important conversation when you're in pain. You are definitely distracted and are not at your best. Treating the ailment, and being cognizant of how it's impacting your work and relationships can help you find ways to mitigate the detrimental effect it can be having on your performance.

Mental fatigue takes away our ability to be a top performer. Constantly working and thinking about work or other challenges is exhausting. Especially in times of conflict or turmoil, not taking a break will impact the other parts of your life and your ability to be your best self. Overthinking and worrying are two ways we unnecessarily give more power to mental stress. Taking time off (even a couple hours), getting exercise, meditating, are all ways to reduce the pressure and not let the mental stress overwhelm you.

Often **environmental** factors are beyond our control and diminish our ability to perform at the level we want. The Great Recession wreaked havoc on so many businesses, leaders, and families in ways that were beyond their control. Whether an economic downturn, a business closing, or changes in your personal life, there are some things we cannot change. What we can decide is how to react when these situations do occur. Do we blame others interminably, fall into the "woe is me" victim mode, and wait for the next terrible thing to happen? Or, do we acknowledge this is the new situation – as lousy as it might be – and push forward to find solutions and opportunities in the chaos?

External **social** factors can be detrimental to our ability to lead ourselves and others, and to live the life we want. The relationships we have with partners, spouses, family members and friends are so important, and also impact every part of our beings. As these relationships follow their normal courses of ups and downs, not being aware of the impact it has on you – or the way you can understand and react to the situation – can diminish your capacity to have the healthy social connections we all desire.

Consciously creating and nurturing social relationships allow us to experience the love, support, and fulfillment needed to navigate a challenging world. How can you rely on the strong relationships during times of stress in the others?

A person's **spiritual** connection is a very personal matter. For some the childhood rituals of church and the community it provides, was an important part of values creation, and perhaps also creating a sense of obligation. Later in life, remaining connected to something bigger and beyond our selves can be an impactful factor in helping give context to the daily challenges we face. When these spiritual connections no longer exist, it can lead to a sense of guilt or purposelessness. Uncovering your spiritual needs, and then seeking to fulfill them can lead to creating a wholeness and contentment, and feeling more control of self.

Emotional stressors are among the most powerful, and debilitating if not identified and acknowledged. The causes of emotional strain can be the result of past decisions we made that we regret and continue to replay. The judgements of self or others about things that are past (and are unchangeable) drain our ability to see things clearly and impact our ability to move forward. Loss of loved ones or jobs causes a sadness that can persist and continue to impact our every day. As we live and work longer, so many individuals are dealing with aging parents and the intense emotional impact that triggers. Having resources to understand and approach these stressors in a helpful manner might include therapists, coaches, and trusted friends.

All of these outside forces are real, and can have a powerful impact on the life of a leader. Any of these can make it difficult to be your best in the workplace or in your personal life. Locating, understanding, and isolating what they are doing to you can help legitimize as well as give clues for how to control the effect they are having on you.

Own the Playing Field

Too often we give up control of a situation by not standing up for what we want, and relinquishing control of the situation.

Another way to think about it is picturing yourself walking onto the football field ready to play. How do you show up so you can own the field? Do you show up without a helmet hoping they go easy on you? No, you show up in full gear ready to hit hard. Do you not have a game plan and just react to what the other team does? No, you have a plan that gives you the confidence you can create the outcome you want. Do you play a weak defense so they continue to walk all over you? No, you show up strong and confident that whatever comes your way you can adapt to stay true to your goals.

You have the confidence to show that you are prepared and are going to play the game to win. You know the rules, you know the opponent, you know what you bring, you can take some blows, and still be confident this is your game to be won.

An executive coaching client, Darren, was consistently frustrated that his boss wasn't appreciating the contribution he was making. Darren had a vision for what his role could be at the company. He tried to initiate conversations around his next steps, and was consistently shut down by his boss.

Digging further, it became apparent Darren wasn't owning the direction of the conversation. His boss would raise an objection, and Darren would get frustrated and focus on the misdirection and get angry, or simply give up. He would walk away complaining about his boss's ignorance.

He was not owning the playing field of the conversation. This was leading to a frustration both emotionally and professionally.

Darren began taking the steps to be able to be clear going into those conversations what he wanted the outcome to be. He didn't want to come away feeling ineffective. He didn't want to be angry. He didn't want to give up control of the conversation – or his career.

He practiced shifting his interpretation of his boss's presumed disrespect or lack of interest so as not to allow it to impact him so personally. He asked more curious questions and respectfully asked for clarifications rather than jumping to conclusions. This allowed Darren to stay in the conversation longer, stand up for himself, and help clarify his wants and needs. His boss now engaged positively in these conversations, and was actually quite ready to help Darren clear up the confusion. He had created assumptions about Darren's leadership skills from these very interactions. When Darren started to own the playing field, his standing in the eyes of his boss improved, and his boss appreciated Darren holding his ground and not giving in to challenging interactions.

By clarifying what success looks like for you in every interaction, you can own the playing field and not walk in blindly. It's not a competition with winners and losers, it's more about the confidence that you can walk into a situation, be present and confident, and not relinquish control unnecessarily. In this way you are able to have more control, and to exhibit leadership qualities.

Owning the Playing Field is not about winners and losers; it's making sure you're showing up with the right equipment and mindset to bring about the outcome you want.

The obstacles described above are ways we give up control of the field. When we hold beliefs or make assumptions or interpretations that are not accurate, or we let our inner critic speak for us, we are relinquishing control.

Step up and realize this is a game you want to compete in and you have more control than you think.

Work-Life Integration

I'm not a fan of the term work-life balance. Of course I know the meaning behind the term and being able to give appropriate time allocations to these two parts of your life is essential.

My concern with the term is it can be seen as a tension between the two; that there is always conflict and you are struggling to please both areas of your life. Or, you might actually be trying to serve two masters, e.g. a boss and a spouse, and that intensifies the potential conflict when you can't seem to satisfy both adequately.

Finding the root cause of what it is that causes our stress, unhappiness, or imbalance helps drive the direction needed to find a better balance. There are often circumstances that are within our control that we ignore or don't want to confront that could help bring into balance that which is causing tension.

I prefer to think of our lives more holistically, and to think of it as *work-life integration.* When we discover our strengths, core values, and goals in all aspects of our lives, we are better to create an integration of both. This helps us to achieve success and creates the lifestyle we want.

John had worked for many years as a senior leader in a marketing company before he became a coaching client. The direction of the company was shifting and he wanted to move on and do something new, either on his own or in another corporate role. An amicable transition with the company was agreed to along with ten months of executive transition coaching.

As I worked with John through this transition – as is the case with most experienced professionals – John was adamant that this next phase of his life had the appropriate balance of work and enjoyment of life. He wanted to feel more in control, and not relinquish the pace and direction of his life to his job. Family was incredibly important to him and he had two children approaching college age. His relationship with his wife was equally important, and not only was he looking at the short term, but wanted to set up a plan to prepare for retirement 10-15 years down the line.

He was seizing the opportunity to use this transition to set a plan in place for happiness and fulfillment, and both career and family were a part of it.

The coaching program was well underway, and summertime was approaching. John was consciously assessing the pros and cons of getting another corporate job or striking out on his own. At this time, we did an exercise where he was able to score eight dimensions of his life on how important they were and how satisfied he was with each one. They included everything from personal relationships, to having fun, to financial success.

Overall, John was doing pretty well with all eight aspects of his life. Those that were most important were on track, and those that were less important weren't requiring much attention. What did jump out at him, however, was an imbalance when it came to the family/parenting dimension. He realized the job search and career discernment process was taking him away from his family. He had been so consumed with his own direction, he failed to realize he was unnecessarily chewing up valuable time with his family, and it was summertime! This was when he had the greatest opportunity to connect with his family, and think about how he wanted the family priority to be integrated with his next career move.

John opted to slow his job search for the summer. He committed to being present in the family activities and trips already planned. He was open to sharing more about his own fears and dreams of what's next with his kids, while trusting his wife to be a valued partner in these crucial next steps.

He didn't abandon the job search over the summer, but integrated it with other priorities so that a foundation was being laid for the future that respected all aspects of his life, and didn't arbitrarily compartmentalize them. This avoided the problem of feeling the dimensions were in conflict, and instead were complimentary.

This experience was important for John as he continued to explore his next career move. He realized even the process of doing the job search was causing a tension with his desire to create a lifestyle that valued both family and his professional needs. He now knew that keeping his core values at the top of mind helped to inform all his decisions and how his next move would honor these.

Work-life integration is all about understanding how the personal and professional can come together to support and honor your core values.

What's the Opportunity?

"What's the opportunity?" is one of my favorite mantras. When challenging situations arise, asking this question helps to mitigate the impact of the four obstacles discussed above. The situation is happening; how do I want to handle it?! I can become timid, get angry, blame others, overanalyze, or use the skills I have to address it. As I tell clients, unless someone's coming at you with a gun or a knife, there's not a lot you can't handle. (And I have had especially talented clients who say even weapons wouldn't be a problem!) When you look at everything that occurs as an opportunity, you are activating the creative, aspirational part of your executive brain (prefrontal cortex), and can find solutions. This is what makes it fun.

I led a team of about 15 extremely talented researchers at one point in my career. We had ambitious revenue goals, and were getting a lot of attention from the senior management team. We had an opportunity to vastly increase our impact.

One of the things I would say as we took on a new client, were dealing with a particularly difficult situation, or were getting crushed under the workload of our own success, was, "This is going to be fun." My team members would look at me and shake their heads. How can this possibly be fun? We're up against it here.

I knew each team member was committed to the goals and vision of the team. I followed the mantra of "play to people's strengths" so they were doing what they did best, and feeling good about it. This delegation and notion of shared success helped the team achieve things no one thought we could.

When I left the team to move into another division, the gift they gave me was a clock that still sits above my desk with the inscription, *"Tim: Thanks for Always Making It Fun. – The Custom Panel Team."* That's one of the greatest compliments a leader can receive: helping drive success while creating a culture of fun along with a lot of hard work. We took control of the situation and, despite challenges, came out on top.

Confidence creates the life you want.

Confidence drives the ability to take control of your life. You want the confidence to be reflective and self-aware so you are able to identify what's really important to you and why. Confidence drives the ability to tell your boss or partner when something is out of balance. Being able to look at challenges as opportunities takes a confidence that you can handle it.

You don't have to resort to the old methods of assigning blame, getting angry, or feeling like a victim. None of those actions will bring about positive results, or allow you to create the life you want.

Start by looking at which of the obstacles or influencers might be getting in your way and take baby steps to overcome them.

Take Care of Yourself

The obstacles described above can be addressed more easily when you are dialed into what your mind and body needs, and are willing to do what it takes to meet those physical and emotional needs.

Early in my career I ran community-based group homes for teenagers with emotional and intellectual disabilities in the mountains of Western Massachusetts, and the inner city of Philadelphia. Living in the home with the teens, the goal was to help them learn the daily living skills that would allow them to achieve the highest degree of independence as they grew up.

When working on behavioral improvement, it was critical to understand what motivated each person so that the positive reinforcement delivered helped them learn the appropriate social and practical skills. Each resident had skills they were working on whether it be hygiene, controlling anger, cleaning their room, respecting others, etc. Similarly, the reinforcement for accomplishing growth in these areas was customized for the individual. The rewards included more TV time, favorite snacks, time alone, extra trips to the store, spending time with the Family Teachers, and so much more. If you offered a reinforcement that wasn't meaningful to the individual, there was no incentive to change behavior.

The same is true for us. What do we do to bring about positive change for ourselves, and what is the positive reinforcement we give ourselves to make it happen?

Taking care of yourself includes knowing what you need, how to make it happen, and creating the rewards to make it stick.

How do take care of yourself effectively to be strong as you encounter the challenges along the way? What do you really need to help you be the complete person you want to be? What are the activities and rewards that motivate you to live the life you want?

The United States is notorious for offering so little paid vacation time for its workers. Entrepreneurs have to work crazy hours to achieve success. In a challenging job market, employees have to go above and beyond to prove their worth to merely keep their jobs. Raising a family while managing careers creates stress whether a couple or a single parent.

When you take the time to become very aware of what helps you – and what doesn't – you have more motivation to incorporate those behaviors or activities into your life. Intense physical activity might be a tool for some, but not everyone. Meditation could assist some to be at the top of their game, while for others it would be maddening.

Taking care of yourself in the midst of these headwinds is essential. Pick the activities that work, and incorporate them into your life.

Physical activity has a chemical impact on the body through the release of the pleasure hormones. Feeling fit not only helps the ability to function and increases the longevity of your body, but also helps with self-image that contributes to confidence and the ability to handle challenges more effectively.

Time alone can be a great tool to help you refocus and shut out the noise of the office and the home. The time can be spent relaxing, thinking, meditating, journaling, and allowing yourself to be more peaceful.

Prayer and meditation allow the brain to declutter, and help you focus on something outside of yourself. Whether you connect with a higher purpose, or create headspace to be able to identify what really matters, you are intentionally helping your brain's ability to recharge and be more effective.

Taking time away helps you to experience new things, gets you out of the routine, and can be a way to take care of yourself. Whether short or long, near home or far way, getting out of the same old scene allows for the change of pace that generates fresh perspective and renewed enthusiasm for the everyday tasks.

Intentionally attending to relationships can go a long way to create more fun and balance in your life. Relationships often create stressors that show up in ways we don't even recognize. Unsatisfying routines, lack of intimacy, frequent conflict, and drifting apart are all indicators that you might not be taking care of yourself in the context of your relationships. Being connected to others is a primal human need, and having the confidence to take on those challenges with the ones closest to you helps you live a life with more contentment.

Having the confidence to look at your life, and honestly say where you have control and where you don't, is critical to create the life you want. Looking at the things that get in your way – whether real or imagined – and tackling them helps start the path to the fulfillment we all seek. What we choose to engage in to bring about the change and regain control differs for each of us, and identifying those motivational activities that are most meaningful can bring about lasting change.

TAKING ACTION

Identifying and Honoring Your Core Values

It's difficult to have fun and feel whole when your key values are not being honored. When someone says, "I hate my job," it's typically because there is misalignment with one or more of their core values. For instance, "I hate my job because my boss never tells me what I do right and we haven't had a review in forever." This person might very well have a core value of "communication" that is not being honored in this situation. Once identified, she can undertake ways to bring about change. Being aligned with your core values helps you be more content and actually have more fun across your relationships and roles.

> ➢ Values Exercise

>> ➢ Below is a list of Personal and Professional Core Values
>> ➢ Select the 10 that are most important to you. You get to define them however you want! Someone might think of communication, for instance, very differently than you. That's ok. What matters is what they mean to you.
>> ➢ Now, take each of those 10 values and write a couple sentences of "what this value means to you." Really spend some time thinking about it.
>> ➢ Now, from those 10, pick the 5 that are really, really the most important to you.
>> ➢ What surprises you about the 5 that rose to the top?

Create a separate page for three key areas of your life: Family, Workplace, Social Life. Now look at each of those 5 Core Values and reflect on how you are, and are not, honoring those values in each of those three areas of your life. If, for instance, "Fun" is one of your values, and you realize you are not finding time to maintain relationships in your social circles, you might not be honoring that value. We are typically unhappy when we are in some way not living up to our core values.

Create an action plan for how you want to maintain and realign your core values in these key areas of your life. What do you want to do? When do you want to begin?

CORE VALUES

Authenticity	Kindness
Achievement	Knowledge
Adventure	Leadership
Authority	Learning
Autonomy	Love
Balance	Loyalty
Beauty	Meaningful Work
Boldness	Openness
Compassion	Optimism
Communication	Peace
Challenge	Pleasure
Citizenship	Poise
Community	Popularity
Competency	Recognition
Contribution	Religion
Creativity	Reputation
Curiosity	Respect
Determination	Responsibility
Fairness	Security
Faith	Self-Respect
Fame	Service
Friendships	Spirituality
Fun	Stability
Growth	Success
Happiness	Status
Honesty	Trustworthiness
Humor	Wealth
Influence	Wisdom
Inner Harmony	Other: _____
Justice	

Chapter 8

The Four Faces of Confidence

*You will know (the good from the bad) when
you are calm, at peace. A Jedi uses the Force
for knowledge and defense, never for attack.*
Yoda

*You decide how you show up. You decide
how you feel when it's over.*
Tim Ressmeyer

Confidence is the most essential component of successful leadership. You can't control the other person; you can only control you. You decide at the end of an interaction, meeting, event, or speech how you feel. No matter what happened, you control your reaction.

It's too easy to say, "I want to be more confident." That's a hard undertaking. There are parts of our lives where it's easier to be confident, and those where it's more of a challenge.

So far in this book we've looked at seven essential dimensions of professional and personal lives where an understanding of confidence can create the success and fulfillment you want. As a leader, creating connections, or going through change, confidence is an important driver of achieving the outcome you want.

It's complicated to remember all the different components of confidence across this myriad of aspects of our lives where we benefit – or are challenged by – confidence. Creating a simple framework to remember the tenets of confidence that lead to success as a leader is a way to remember, apply, and maintain these behaviors. In other words, a tool to help *generalize* to other situations.

The Four Faces of Confidence can serve that purpose. When you picture yourself in different situations, you can use this framework to help yourself answer the question, "How do I want to show up?" Each of the faces represent choice you can make as you step into a situation whether it seems to be life-altering or more mundane.

Each of the faces is not inherently good or bad. There are different times where a different approach is most appropriate. In the brief descriptions that follow, all those nuances will not be addressed, and you will see there is definitely a bias towards which ones will be most impactful. Know that the faces that are covered in a less positive fashion do have their benefits.

Face 1 – The Passive

The Passive Face is the face where you choose to sit back and observe. You don't step in or engage. It may be a conscious choice, or it may be a lack of confidence that you can or want to have an impact.

The Passive Face of confidence can be helpful for understanding the landscape of a company and avoiding conflict. This can be effective during times of major change, or perhaps when just stepping into a new role. Adopting this style of leadership for a longer period of time can lead to an inability to advance, as you are likely abdicating leadership and taking control of your path.

This face can be an indication someone is lacking in confidence for a host of reasons. They let old experiences dominate. They have had bad experiences they can't let go of. They sit quietly; agonizingly hearing others say the things they wish they could say. They feel things are just stacked against them, so why try. They show up in meetings, interviews, or in relationships already expecting they cannot make a difference, but wishing they could.

Sometimes this is the result of things that have happened in the past, or the way they view themselves. Perhaps you label yourself as an introvert. You don't feel you can come up with comments or answers as quickly as the extroverts around you. As a result, you don't even try. Sometimes you say, *yes* in the moment when asked to do something, because you couldn't say "let me think about it" fast enough. You walk away feeling lousy because you didn't engage in the moment. Or, you go up to the leader after the meeting and offer your opinions, and they're wondering why you didn't speak up in the moment.

Think about how that feels. How will people around you (boss, coworker, client, friend) respond to you if you are showing up with this kind of view of yourself? How true is it that you have to show up this way? Sometimes there are things that are stacked against you, but how effective is it showing up this way? Do you do it more frequently than you would like?

Adam, had a mid to high level role in a small, and growing, tech-based company. He had success elsewhere in his career, but things were hitting a snag as the company was expecting more and more from him. He had a very passive approach to his work. He expected those around him to know he was capable, and hoped his gentle asks for collaboration would get the enthusiastic response he wanted. They weren't. Everyone was busy, and for him to get his job done successfully, he had to engage others across the organization with more energy and enthusiasm.

The senior management team at the company hired me to work with him along with other leaders as they were navigating this critical juncture in their growth. They wanted to make sure they had the best people in the key areas of responsibility, the high performers were being supported, those who needed more help were receiving that assistance, and others were being evaluated to see whether they were the right fit for the company. Everyone was being treated respectfully, and a true effort was being made to create the best possible outcomes.

Time was spent working with Adam to see what it would take for him to step up and execute within the role that was needed. Adam admitted it was a confidence challenge for him, and he realized there wasn't enough motivation for him to change his behavior within this organization. It was mutually decided that the company was not a good fit for him, and he and the company were best served if he was to move on.

Adam's passive approach to his role was a combination of a lack of confidence that he could deliver against what was expected in that particular environment, and identifying where he really wanted to focus his energy. The company provided coaching through his transition to help him uncover that passion to set him up for success in the job search and he was able to find a job that was a much better fit, and continued coaching helped him move into a more confident style of leadership.

Face 2 - The Mediator

The Mediator looks at all sides. Over and over. You are always trying to please everyone involved. This can be helpful in times of conflict and you can serve others who by being level-headed. You can serve the role of diplomat.

If there's been a problem, you're willing to admit where you might have some responsibility. You see where you can give and take. You're willing to compromise. You help others try to figure things out, too. Sometimes you win, sometimes you lose. And, that's ok.

On the down side, it might feel good to find common ground, to be fair all the time, but you aren't truly satisfied. You're getting some of what you want, but not all, and you can't fully let go of that. Especially if this happens frequently, it always feels the other guys are getting more of what they want than you are.

This is very common in the business world when you feel more natural as a collaborator, but those around you are much more driven to make all the moves.

It doesn't come naturally to be more direct, so you rely on your interpersonal skills to help everyone come to the table and help you make the decision. It helps, but it can still impact your ability to learn the skills of owning a decision and making it happen.

Karen was one of the principals in a family-owned business. Those organizations, just by the nature of the familial relationships, have a unique set of challenges and opportunities. I was working with the leadership team of which she was part. She filled the role of mediator at work as she probably did growing up as well. There was volatility between family members as they made strategic decisions about the future of the company. Dad was nearing retirement, and the next generation had to step up to take the lead of selling, growing, or maintaining the company.

Karen served a very valuable role in helping to see all sides of the issues, and had the confidence to step in and help everyone be heard, and to keep people focused on what was important. The old patterns of conflict were obvious between certain family members, and Karen was always able to help soothe the egos, and keep things moving forward.

The role was important, and she exercised it well.

There was a downside as well. Being the mediator and the one who always had to keep the company on track added pressure to her life, and she didn't feel she was appreciated as a leader. Always working in the middle of the family dynamics, she hadn't fully developed leadership – and confidence – skills that would allow her to get what she wanted both personally and professionally. She would always be a participant in the leadership, but wasn't seen as President or CEO material. This role where she was always helping others get along spilled over into her personal life where she felt the company was taking up too much of her time, and she resented everyone's assumption that she could always drop everything to serve the organization.

This role was important, and she was good at it, but it had led Karen into a place she didn't want to be. Through coaching she became aware of the way in which there were assumptions she and the others were making that were impacting her effectiveness. She began to establish clearer boundaries for herself, and did not feel she always had to wear the Mediator Face. She wasn't responsible for always putting out the fires and helping people get along, others had to own this as well.

She began to use the other faces of confidence in order to expand her impact, make herself feel more valued each day, and to establish a significant position for herself as part of the company's strategic planning.

The Mediator can inhibit their ability to move forward because of a lack of decisiveness. They are such a pleaser, they have trouble making a decision and being clear. They are seen as valuable on a team, but not always viewed as a strong leader who can push forward or gain a following.

Face 3 - The Aggressor

The Aggressor is seen as definitive. They are clear about what they want and they let everyone know it. They get stuff done, because there's no room for opposing viewpoints or other options.

This is a very valuable face to wear in certain settings, or at periods when there just is not enough time for a conversation to take place. Some decisions have to be made quickly, and with confidence.

Frank was a senior leader responsible for operations at a manufacturing plant. His default confidence was that of an Aggressor. He oversaw people on the floor of the plant who had to get stuff done, and there was always a myriad of risks around health, safety, and employee relations. He also played an integral role on the leadership team, and had strong feelings, and motivations, to make sure the rest of the leadership team knew exactly how he felt things were being done. This Aggressor Face extended beyond his own areas of responsibility.

He did get stuff done and the company was successful, but Frank was not happy. He exhausted himself and everyone around him. Everything was always a battle and no one ever measured up to his expectations. The yelling, negativity, and bullying was taking its toll throughout the company.

Frank was a textbook example of the downside of the Aggressor. If this is happening all the time, the Aggressor is actually limiting their effectiveness. They often lack confidence or knowledge and are over-compensating by being aggressive. They're always right. A bully. He wouldn't listen to challenges or alternatives. Aggressors get stuff done, but could do even more without draining others. They aren't fully optimizing their own creativity, nor the talent around them. They create more conflict that ultimately takes more time and energy to clean up the messes.

We see this type of confidence throughout the workforce. It's the bully or, if less dramatic, the know-it-all leadership that is so prevalent. It's seen in established companies, small businesses, and startups. It also shows up in interpersonal relationships.

The Aggressor has a need to continue to prove to all those around them they have all the answers. They don't want – or know how – to constructively deal with soliciting ideas from others, or making mistakes and rebounding. Instead they just push through with their own agenda. Confidence is often hanging in the balance for the Aggressor because the consequences of failure are great, since they have heaped so much responsibility on themselves.

Sadly, people tend to not want to follow an Aggressor for long because those impacted are not contributing at the level they are capable of, and are exhausted by the lack of trust shown to them.

In working with Frank, the coaching focused on how to distribute some of the tasks he was doing that could be done by others. This would help to reduce his stress level and a feeling that he was the only one who could get things done. In working with the workers on the floor of the plant, Frank learned skills of leadership development that would allow others to feel valued and respected. This cut down on the conflict he was experiencing, and created growth paths for these workers to step into roles that could ultimately build their skill set. In working with the other leaders responsible for other parts of the business, he was able to reduce his judgment of their domains, and serve more as a strategic collaborator.

There is need for decisive leadership, and wearing the Aggressor face can help drive that. Often the confidence that is being shown is in fact not very deep, and the behavior is likely covering up areas where there is a *lack* of confidence and an inadequate understanding of how to build and grow talent of others.

Face 4 - The Creator

The Creator sees every situation as an opportunity. They know they have strengths and can deliver value and impact. Even in tough situations they are confident they can find solutions to bring about an outcome they want. They keep moving things forward by leveraging their strengths, and they don't have to try too hard to prove their worth to others.

One of these strengths is a confidence to listen and learn from others. They do not have to believe (or pretend) they are the smartest person in the room. They know there are those around them who can contribute to a challenging situation; it doesn't have to be only them.

They are not afraid to make mistakes or come up with ideas that might seem crazy. They understand that unleashing their own creativity – and encouraging the same from those around them – can lead to solutions they never could have come up with if they were feeling like a victim, trying to please everyone, or making decisions as a bully.

They also know that decisions have to be made, and they're not afraid to take a stand, knowing that if things don't work out as planned they are able to work to handle that next situation.

Seeing a Creator in action is truly a gift. As you look back over your career and think of the people you admire or want to model your own behavior after, they are likely exhibiting those characteristics of a Creator.

Through training as a professional coach I learned to see those things that get in the way of people – myself included – from becoming the leaders they can be. So much of it comes down to identifying and getting rid of the obstacles that break down our confidence. When we realize we have more control than we think, and the consequences are far less than we imagine, we can move forward more confidently.

Freeing yourself from the fear and self-imposed limitations creates the opportunity to be the person you want to be, and do the things you want to do.

You have the freedom to create!

TAKING ACTION

Create a page with the Four Faces of Confidence (Victim, Mediator, Aggressor, Creator) as headings. Underneath each, write situations, jobs, personal relationships, or interactions where the way you show up reflects that face. Be honest. Be thorough. Take time to really reflect and make as an exhaustive list as you can.

Now look at that list:

> ➤ Look for patterns in the experiences that fall in each category.
> ➤ How satisfied are you in how you present yourself in these situations?
> ➤ Where do you tend to show more confidence, and where is there likely to be less? Why is that?
> ➤ Reflect on each of the faces, put yourself in that real situation, and to the best of your ability, think about how you *feel* in the moment. What feels empowering and exciting? What feels draining, embarrassing, or fearful?

Now create an action plan for what you want to do differently moving forward. In the first exercise you linked your experiences with the Four Faces of Confidence to feelings. Knowing what feels good – and wanting to replicate it – is one of the greatest motivators we can have. We'd much rather feel great than feel lousy. Use those positive experiences to help craft a plan so you experience more of those, and fewer of the others.

> ➤ List the 5 experiences from the list above where you felt you were feeling the best.

> > ➤ What did that feel like?

> ➤ What are the characteristics of those experiences that helped me feel great? What did I go in with in order to have that confidence?

> ➤ List the 5 experiences that didn't feel so great.

> ➤ What happened?
> ➤ If I were to have that experience all over again, what would I like to do differently?

> ➤ From this list and exercise write three words or phrases (mantras) you want to use to remind yourself when you're walking into those situations where you're not feeling great or have struggled in the past.

As I was starting my coaching business, confidence was definitely something I had to practice on a daily basis. I was starting something new and I wasn't sure how it was going to work out. My coaches helped me develop the mantras that helped me succeed. As examples for this part of the exercise, here are mine:

> ➤ Be Tim!
> ➤ Blaze Your Trail!
> ➤ Be Big!
> ➤ You Know How to Do This!
> ➤ It's Your Time Now!

Chapter 9

Conclusion

You are braver than you believe, stronger than you seem, and smarter than you think.
A.A. Milne

*Leadership is being the person others want to follow so they can accomplish things they couldn't do on their own, and it all begins with **confidence**.*
Tim Ressmeyer

There's no question in my mind that confidence is foundational to the success of any leader. Remember, we are all leaders, leaders of ourselves first and foremost. You decide how you want to show up, no matter what has happened. You can't always control the situation – or the other person – you can control your response.

Showing up confidently is easier in some situations than others. When clients share that they just want more confidence, my heart aches, because I know what that feels like. We all have areas where we feel great and others where we just wish we could get unstuck or handle things differently.

Being a social scientist at my core, I love to understand why people do the things they do, and what are the factors that influence the actions they take. Also being a behaviorist, I believe that behaviors can be learned, and therefore unlearned. New behaviors can be practiced to replace the ones that aren't working for you. An eternal optimist that individuals can lead happy lives, I very much weigh in on the side of nurture in the nature/nurture dichotomy. You can do things to bring about the change you want. I believe there are very few things that are hardwired or that fall into the bucket, "well, that's just the way I am."

Admittedly, this is a very intellectual or cognitive perspective, while confidence can be very emotional. Can we really *think* our way into more confidence? Here we get into the head vs. heart debate. Interestingly, neuroscience research points to us having five brains. One of the five is the heart brain where we have the "gut feel" whether or not we feel safe in a situation, and can therefore move forward, or back away and avoid something we do not want to confront. It sounds a lot like confidence to me.

When you realize you are not feeling safe, or are not connecting, you can discover what is triggering that reaction. Is it real or imagined? How can you tap into past experiences to see how you handled it effectively in the past?

We are in fact able to create new pathways within our brain(s), and create aspirational outcomes that can help overcome the limitations which are both real and imagined. We have a storehouse of experiences and emotions that can be activated to help move us forward. And, we have the executive brain function that coordinates the entire brain, and allows us to envision a future where we are living productively, and aligned with our values and goals.

The work of this book has been to show how confidence shows up in seven key areas of a leader's life: leadership, passion, connecting, change, advancement, relationships, and control. From my own experience in leadership roles, plus the exposure to countless examples in the lives of my colleagues and clients, being confident in these situations leads to success.

The Taking Action exercises at the end of each chapter are designed to help you look closely at how you are doing right now in these key areas. In so many you are doing great! Leverage those strengths and build on those successes as you also recognize the areas you can have a greater impact. The Action Plan steps are designed to help you create new pathways, both intellectually and emotionally to move forward and find that success, happiness, and fulfillment.

To help you walk away with a simple framework to remember, Chapter 8 introduced the Four Faces of Confidence. You can decide which face you *choose* to wear as you move through your day or life. Do you want to be a Passive, Mediator, Aggressor, or Creator? You have more choice than you might think.

Confidence is an attribute that is squishy and hard to define and put your finger on. You know it when you see it, and it's hard to create when you don't feel like you have it. It can be built, however, and once you do, the ***impact of confidence*** can make all the difference.

About the Author

Tim Ressmeyer, Ph.D. is a Certified Professional Coach (CPC) and holds additional accreditations from the International Coach Federation (ICF) as a Professional Certified Coach (PCC), and from the Conversational Intelligence® for Coaches he has earned the Enhanced Practitioner Certification (C-IQ). Tim is the Founding Partner of Ressmeyer Partners and Happy Hour Coach® which provides life, leadership and executive coaching services globally. As a coach, author, workshop leader, and speaker he works with individuals, leadership teams, and organizations to bring about personal and professional excellence. He is frequently quoted in Forbes, and was a contributor at WGN Radio in Chicago. His professional career also includes serving in direct care and management roles for nonprofits, a university faculty member, and 20 years as a corporate senior executive in major market research and advertising companies.

CPSIA information can be obtained
at www.ICGtesting.com
Printed in the USA
BVHW04*1153260818
524429BV00016B/5/P